Praise for *Diamond Highway:*

"Tony Cape's *Diamond Highway* is a compellingly-written, searingly honest memoir of his life and times as a student, at once doubting and devoted, of the brilliant and provocative Tibetan Buddhist master Chogyam Trungpa Rinpoche, and his controversial successor Vajra Regent Osel Tendzin.

"Unlike previous memoirs, Cape deals head on with both of his teachers' unconventional sexual and drinking behaviors, as well as the tragic and disturbing events surrounding the Regent's death from AIDS only three years after the early death of Trungpa Rinpoche.

"The personal journey that Tony Cape vividly describes in Diamond Highway is, above all, a journey of growing self-awareness. He pulls no punches in sharing both the highs and the lows of the path and the debilitating anguish of his several episodes of major depression. This gritty first-person account will serve equally well to introduce newcomers to the extraordinary career of Chogyam Trungpa Rinpoche and to give readers with similar life experiences occasion to reflect deeply on the events and the meaning of their own journeys."

> David Rome
> Private secretary to Chogyam Trungpa, Rinpoche
> Co-founder, *Embodied Listening*

"An amazingly sensitive portrayal of what our life was like with Trungpa Rinpoche and the Vajra regent."

> Lodro Dorje
> Loppon of the Three Yana Studies
> Vajradhatu International

"...a page-turner. *Diamond Highway* is a portrait of Trungpa Rinpoche of which we can be proud."

> Acharya Larry Mermelstein
> Senior teacher
> Executive Director, Nalanda Translation Committee

"I highly recommend this book as the best current work on this subject."

> John Perks
> former head of household for Chögyam Trungpa, Rinpoche

DIAMOND HIGHWAY

A Tibetan Buddhist
Path in America

Tony Cape

DIAMOND HIGHWAY
A Tibetan Buddhist Path in America

Cover Art Design: John Johnston, Hans Teensma

Author Photograph: Chip Weems

Edited by: Rosie Pearson, Positive Proof Editing
Website: www.editorrosie.net

Printed and Distributed by: Off-the-Commons Books
Website: www.collectivecopies.coop

ISBN: 978-1-937146-29-0

Printed in U.S.A.

10 9 8 7 6 5 4 3 2 1

diamond highway

By the same author

The Cambridge Theorem
The Last Defector
Triple Cross
Blood Ties

for Wendy

I saw a highway of diamonds with nobody on it.

Bob Dylan
"Hard Rain"
1962

prologue

It is the kindest face I have ever seen—open, playful and wise. It is round and copper-colored, with small, wide-set eyes behind heavy, old-fashioned lenses.

What are your plans? he asks me in formally accented English.

I have to go back to England, I say. *But I'd like to come back here and study with you, if I can.*

Write to me and I'll help you, he responds quietly.

The interview is apparently over because someone is helping me stand. I squeeze the soft brown hand with gratitude and he smiles. Outside the tent I am besieged by people I have met the previous week.

What'd he say? You gonna' stay? Hey, he really likes you!

My life has just changed decisively, and I can think of nothing relevant to say. But I am bounteously, gluttonously happy, and I'm sure it shows.

He is Chögyam Trungpa, Rinpoche, maverick Tibetan lama, counterculture heavyweight and in this era—the year is 1976—the most dynamic and controversial buddhist[1] teacher in the West. I am a twenty-something British itinerant, a dissatisfied idealist curious about Eastern spirituality, but as yet unable to find commitment in work or relationships. In other words, we are a perfect fit.

Subsequently, I would go on to become Rinpoche's student and one of his *kusung* or personal attendants (a position of great privilege) until his death in 1987.

---

[1] Throughout this account, I do not capitalize the terms "buddhism" or "buddhist." Buddhism is not a religion in the Oxford dictionary definition of the term—"recognition...of some higher unseen power as having control of...destiny, and as being entitled to obedience, reverence, and worship." Buddhism does not posit any such extrinsic power. In Sanskrit the term buddha means simply "the awakened one."

I offer this memoir for several reasons. Firstly, I wish to express my love and gratitude to my teacher Trungpa Rinpoche, whose teaching has had a profound influence on my life and on the lives of many others. By recounting my own experiences as his student I hope to add to the portrait that other memoirs and biographies have begun to shape and perhaps provide inspiration to those interested in exploring his teachings. Secondly, I want to discuss his legacy and address some of the questions that arise from his controversial lifestyle and teaching methods. And lastly, because I suffer from the mental illness of depression, I want to share my particular experience as a dharma student with this disorder.

Some further context: Asking pointed questions has been a practice of mine throughout my life, particularly in public forums—it is something I feel compelled to do. No doubt a primary reason is self-aggrandizement—I want to show that I'm clever and have a way with words. However, a secondary and, I hope, redeeming motive is that I believe that asking tough questions can be helpful in clarifying important issues for others. The several accounts of Chögyam Trungpa's life that have been published to date all acknowledge the issues of his sexuality and drinking, but to my mind, none examines the specific repercussions for our community during his lifetime or for his legacy today. As interest in buddhism in the West continues to grow, many people who are attracted to Chögyam Trungpa's teachings may nevertheless be disturbed by the seeming contradictions of his private life. It is in the spirit of promoting clarity and openness that I ask these questions about my teacher's life.

Finally, as someone who has suffered from major depression all my adult life, I am intimately familiar with the isolation that is one of its peculiar horrors. However, during periods when reading any printed matter is an ordeal, the one genre that can compel attention is depression narrative, because such stories convey the vital knowledge that the sufferer is not alone and that recovery is possible. In part because of the stigma that attaches to mental illness, most of us endure our depressive episodes in secret. I offer my own experiences as an expression of solidarity with all those whose lives have been touched by this appalling affliction.

one

My interview with Chögyam Trungpa, Rinpoche comes at the end of a week-long meditation program at his retreat center in the Colorado Rockies. (Rinpoche is what everyone, at this juncture, calls him. It's a Tibetan honorific, meaning "Precious One," pronounced RIN-po-chay.) I have ended up here through a series of seeming accidents, although when I picked Boulder, Colorado as my destination on leaving the New Mexico commune, I knew that Trungpa Rinpoche lived there. I also knew it was the site of Naropa Institute, the ultra-hip college he had started and where Allen Ginsberg, William Burroughs, and Ram Dass taught. (And after all, his scary book, *Cutting Through Spiritual Materialism*, is the single volume I have brought with me from England on this trip to the States.) So perhaps our encounter is more aptly termed "auspicious coincidence," a notion I will later learn is central to the Tibetan buddhist view of the spiritual path.

Toward the end of the program, at which Rinpoche gives evening talks on the life of the eleventh-century Indian buddhist saint Naropa, he has deliberately—so it seems to me and others—teased and played with me, so our interview is really the culmination of a process that began earlier in the week. Naturally, I have been flattered by this attention, although I sense it is due in large part to my Englishness, a quality that is obvious as soon as I open my mouth. This I have contrived to do at my earliest opportunity, partly to clarify a point he has made but more deliberately to initiate some kind of interaction with him. I find him enthralling, and as I mentioned earlier, I have never been timid about putting myself forward in this way.

Rinpoche's talks are based on the biography of Naropa, a venerated scholar at the vast monastic college of Nalanda in northern India.

Naropa's true spiritual journey begins after a toothless hag visits him in his cell and calls him a liar when he claims to know both the sense and inner meaning of the Buddha's teachings. She admonishes him that he needs to study with her brother Tilopa, an eccentric yogi, to understand their true meaning. On hearing Tilopa's name, Naropa is overwhelmed with devotion and sets out to find him. (Tilopa and Naropa became the Indian progenitors of what would later be called the Kagyu or Oral Lineage, one of the four schools of buddhism in Tibet.) In his talk, Rinpoche surveys the highlights of Naropa's quest, but he uses these events as a springboard to present the pitfalls of the spiritual path in general, and those governed by the compulsion of ego in particular. His eloquence is dazzling—he speaks in a distinct Oxonian accent with an offbeat syntax—and his language is extravagant, slangy and often hilarious. At the end of his second talk, Rinpoche is asked why Naropa had to abandon his wife in order to search for his teacher Tilopa. He smiles broadly and explains that Naropa was denied the "funky wisdom" of the twentieth century, which allows women the equality to practice carpentry and go to war with real weapons instead of rolling pins. His shoulders rock with laughter at this notion, as they often do. In fact, his whole presence is subversive, iconoclastic. He is a small, solid man with thick black hair and flat Asian features who wears safari suits or occasionally a bulbous Shetland cardigan at his evening talks. He sits in an ornately patterned armchair, sipping alcohol from an antique cocktail glass as if on the set of a Vincent Price movie. He is the most extraordinary person I have ever seen.

Naropa's trials include encounters with all manner of revolting creatures, including a leper woman and a stinking, maggot-infested dog. Naropa reacts with predictable aversion and, time and again, the apparition vanishes into a rainbow, leaving Naropa swooning on a sandy plateau. Rinpoche's gloss on these events is compelling. He alludes to Naropa's arrogance and aggression in his search for his teacher, which entails "rejecting the feminine principle and rejecting your own shit…People searching for the guru are looking for something pure, better and automatically reject what doesn't meet their expectations. When you realize there is something profound in the teachings, you begin to experience some sense that you don't like what you are, that you are going to change into something else by finding a scapegoat. But one has to experience one's own dirtiness—*duhkha*."

This is the first time I have heard this Sanskrit term, usually translated as "suffering," the First Noble Truth of the Buddha's vast teachings. When Naropa finally drops his attachment to both his preconceptions and his social and intellectual status, Tilopa appears to him in human form and accepts him as his student. Nevertheless many ordeals await Naropa after he becomes Tilopa's student and gradually sheds the carapace of his egotism. He is still given to extreme reactions, which include pounding his erect penis with a rock after taking a consort on his teacher's suggestion, and then resolving to commit suicide in order to study with Tilopa in a future lifetime. Finally Naropa attains enlightenment when Tilopa slaps him in the face with his sandal, a particularly humiliating insult among Indians. This theme that runs through Naropa's life of the suffering caused by pride and self-deception strikes a strong chord in me.

In his second-to-last talk, in commenting on Naropa's repeated failure to treat Tilopa's more grotesque manifestations with respect, Rinpoche has said, *The student should not badmouth the teacher, and the teacher should not badmouth the student.* During the question period, I raise my hand, and, when called upon, ask whether this statement implies suspending the student's critical intelligence. (For some reason, my critical intelligence feels like my most valuable asset at this juncture of my life. Plus, I don't follow his logic. Is he implying that healthy skepticism is the same thing as looking for a scapegoat?)

Rinpoche turns his profile away from me, gazing at the ceiling of the large tent in which we meditate and listen to his talks. His expression is one of fatigue.

Originally, the British sense of humor is wretched, he says—taking particular relish in enunciating the word "wretched." (Scattered gasps and titters from the audience.)

He turns to look at me sternly over his spectacles. Americans have a far better sense of humor in their uncultured way, he says. (More laughter.)

And then he takes another question.

My face grows hot. Was my question really that dumb? Is he serious? Rinpoche is unfailingly polite, even to the trippiest of students. Why is he being mean to me? Or is he?

Later in the question period Rinpoche appears to relent, or at least signal his playfulness. In response to a guy who makes a convoluted point about the teacher, the student and grains of sand, Rinpoche agrees, then claims that the grains have Union Jacks on them, turns to me, and waves. This brings gales of laughter to the room and elation to my heart. Another question about devotion is rejected as too complicated. Make it more simple, jokes Rinpoche, without the Union Jack on it.

By the end of the talk I'm both thrilled and embarrassed by this banter. During the discussion group next day (there are perhaps two hundred of us at the program, split into groups of fifteen or so for discussion) people ask me what I have made of these exchanges. My response is that, like Naropa, I looked for a sandy plateau to swoon on. People laugh and offer their own interpretations, but I have this strong hunch that Naropa, a highly intelligent but conceited student who consistently misses the point because of his arrogance and preconceptions, is indeed me. Me? I came here knowing next to nothing about buddhism or spirituality. But I do know as the week progresses that I have fallen hard for this adorable man called Chögyam Trungpa. On the program's last afternoon I decide to join the line of students waiting for a private word with him. I would probably have waited several days if necessary.

When it is my turn, I kneel in front of his teaching chair and put my hands on his knees. He is wearing a khaki outfit with shorts, so this is an intimate gesture on my part, but I want to touch him, feel his flesh. He smiles and asks me my name.

As happens many times subsequently, outer phenomena fall away when I talk to Rinpoche. I enter the magical, protected space of his regard and experience a communication more intimate than I have ever known. We speak a little about England and where I am from in Yorkshire. Rinpoche, of course, has visited my hometown. I ask him when he might be returning to England, and tell him there are many people there who would appreciate his teaching. Rinpoche tells me he has no plans to return, ever, that there is much more space in America. As a fellow Englishman (bizarre that Rinpoche, born in a nomad's tent on the

Tibetan plateau, always felt to me like a fellow Englishman), I know exactly what he means. We are not talking about geography. It is then that he asks me my plans, and we share the exchange with which I began my story.

But I was evasive in my reply to Rinpoche, and it is appropriate that I explain why. In fact, I have no pressing obligation to return to England at this time. I am unattached and unemployed, and I think America is an exhilarating place. Rinpoche is a magnetic individual, and his students seem like my natural peers—mostly my age, intelligent, skeptical, and funny. But I feel I must escape, for prudence' sake, because I am on the rebound. I have just broken up with a woman I have been with for four years, my first serious lover. And now I have just fallen in love again, almost immediately, which I find fishy. Although I seriously doubt it, Trungpa Rinpoche might be a charlatan and his community might be a cult. Later I will understand that falling in love romantically and falling in love with a guru are similar experiences. But for now I distrust my own enthusiasm and make plans to leave.

The encounter with Rinpoche was the capstone of a thrilling week for me, and I was truly elated as I drove away from the Rocky Mountain Dharma Center after that seminar in 1976. On my departure, I felt I had made sufficient connection to already consider myself a buddhist, but this conviction felt like it was due more to the joy of recognition than the rapture of conversion. Hearing Rinpoche teach about the folly of the great, learned Naropa, I had found myself continually saying to myself, *Right. Of course. Yes, sure, that has to be it*—Naropa's preconceptions inhibit the direct experience of reality and make him afraid. Well, that's true for me, too, obviously; it's true for everyone. These cascading connections left me somewhat giddy after the evening talks, a state that was continually undercut by the requirement to do many hours of meditation practice the following day.

The power of Rinpoche's approach at the Naropa seminar (I would later learn it distinguished his entire approach to the presentation of buddhism in the West) was that he combined his own lucid exposition with an insistence that his students commit to extensive sitting meditation practice. Crucially, instruction in meditation technique was pro-

vided through private interview with an experienced teacher who was
also a student of Rinpoche. This requirement had the dramatic effect of
allowing me to verify by actual experience the concepts he presented in
his talks. Thus there was never any need for a leap of faith, which had
been a big obstacle during my brief interest in Christianity in my teens.
Either I experienced some measure of calmness, clarity and insight—respite from the struggle of ego—during and after meditation practice, or
I didn't. If I did, then there were major implications for how I typically
constructed meaning in my life, and my resources were actually far
greater than I thought they were. I also sensed that these resources had
been uncovered rather than manufactured, and were therefore intrinsic
if not actually "mine."

I think I'd also unconsciously anticipated that someone who was
genuinely a spokesman for reality would be like Trungpa Rinpoche.
There was no hint of piety about him. Instead, he seemed to find the
predicament of Naropa—and by extension, that of everybody else—
hugely amusing. But there was nothing condescending about him either—he radiated a warmth and kindness that were palpable. As many
people who became his students have recounted, meeting Trungpa
Rinpoche was like recognizing someone you already knew, with whom
you had an extraordinary and longstanding connection.

The Naropa seminar in 1976 was the pivotal week of my life. I'd
gone to RMDC feeling scared by the finality of lost love and uncertain
where to turn next in my life. I left feeling grounded and inspired, confident that I'd made a lasting commitment that would enable all manner
of opportunities (in which Rinpoche's pledge to help me return to his
community surely played a big role.) Looking back thirty-five years
later, this conviction proved accurate. Naïvely, I also assumed that this
new tool of meditation I had learned meant I need never suffer from
bouts of depression again. In this belief, I was to be sorely disappointed.

I likely suffered my first bout of major depression in my early teens,
following a severe stomach flu that left me weak and emaciated. I recall
taking long solitary walks as I tried to regain my strength, feeling bleak
and hopeless and scared. I was an ardent, sensitive young man, precocious and extroverted with a quick and sometimes malicious tongue. I

was also insecure, fearful, and unnaturally attached to my mother. During this period of recuperation I first experienced my lifelong insomnia, lying awake or reading late into repeated nights. And, as also became a lifelong pattern, I spoke to no one about these feelings of hopelessness, and they gradually abated and I returned to school.

I grew up in a small town in the north of England in the 1950s and 60s. Huddersfield is part of that conurbation of old industrial cities in West Yorkshire that includes Leeds, Bradford, and Sheffield and a host of smaller mill towns. My hometown was characterized above all by its keen sense of humor and its acute provincialism; there was even a Huddersfield accent, distinct from that of towns just fifteen miles away. For an ambitious teenager with shallow roots (my elder sister and I were actually born in Wales) in this era, one goal superseded all others—escape. The guarantor of this escape was education, specifically the promise of attending a university, and as an adolescent I threw myself into academic work with neurotic fervor. But there were other styles of escape, particularly of the imagination, and that is how I first learned something of Tibetan buddhism.

My best friend in school was a lugubrious fellow named Martin. In those years before comprehensive education, Martin and I attended the local selective state secondary school. Founded in 1608, King James' Grammar School was a small, deeply traditional place modeled on the exclusive British public school system, with uniforms, houses, prefects and schoolmasters (we were all male) wearing gowns and wielding switches, paddles, and frequently, their bare hands to maintain order. Martin and I were typical intellectual "arty" types—drawn to literature, drama and music, in particular the sounds of Liverpool and San Francisco. Our standard-bearer in these pursuits was Gary, an even more precocious fellow who started poetry magazines, wrote and performed his own songs and even shacked up with a girlfriend in a Pakistani family's house at the age of seventeen.

Gary was an acolyte of The Incredible String Band, an achingly pure quartet of Scottish folk singers and instrumentalists. Their music was mysterious and spiritual and at one of their concerts Gary learned of a place in Scotland called Samye Ling, where Tibetan buddhists lived. Dauntless, Gary first visited alone in 1968 and again with his girlfriend the following year. He returned with tales of exotic Tibetan practices, American women and rumored sightings of titans like Leonard Cohen and John Lennon. Martin and I were engaged on our own adolescent spiritual quest at this time, and our experimentation with séance and the ouija board had led us to a bizarre spiritualist church where local mediums would channel "friends in spirit" who would then deliver banal messages to relatives in the congregation. The place was an odd conflation of Methodist chapel and carnival sideshow, but Martin and I attended faithfully for several months. We had even been "adopted" by a mysterious guy from Eastern Europe who ran a Saturday morning salon in which he held forth on the teachings of Blavatsky, Ouspensky, and Steiner—our inclusion in his discussion group made us feel sophisticated and adult. I was dead set on visiting the mysterious Tibetan place as soon as possible; Martin, a lapsed Christian, was more skeptical. But as with other ambitious ventures for provincial schoolboys in this era— the Isle of Wight festival in 1969 was another prime example—the logistics proved too difficult. Although I made several other attempts to visit in ensuing years, the exotic Tibetans would have to wait seven years before I finally made the trip to visit their Scottish center.

two

As I was fantasizing about how to visit to the exotic Tibetans in the summer of 1968, Chögyam Trungpa, Rinpoche, who had founded the Samye Ling center the previous year, was contemplating a much larger challenge of his own. He had been trained since infancy to assume spiritual leadership of a series of monasteries in Eastern Tibet, as well as to become governor of the region. However, he'd been forced to flee Tibet following the Chinese invasion of 1959, leading a group of refugees on a perilous overland journey into exile in India. Since then, he'd learned English and studied at Oxford University, then founded the meditation center in the Scottish lowlands, where a small group of British students had gathered around him. His challenge was that the transmission of buddhism to Western students was not working well. During a retreat in Bhutan that summer, Rinpoche experienced a crucial insight that was to determine the direction of his teaching for the rest of his life.

Rinpoche knew that the main barrier to the authentic transmission of the Buddha's teaching to Western students was the very exoticism that appealed so strongly to me in this same era. His insight during his retreat at Taktsang in Bhutan was that such exoticism induced a materialistic response on the part of his Western students—not in the ordinary sense of accumulating stuff, but a spiritual materialism that treated the Buddha's teaching as an adornment that enhanced the self. Later in America, Rinpoche would give this impulse toward spiritual materialism his own deathless formulation—"tripping on the tripless trip." But for now, Rinpoche returned to Scotland convinced that he understood the root problem affecting his relationship with Western dharma students, but uncertain of how to proceed. After all, he could hardly erase his identity as an incarnate lama trained in the esoteric tradition of Tibetan buddhism, could he?

Chögyam Trungpa was born in a nomad's tent in February 1940 in Geje, in northeastern Tibet. When he was a year old, monks from Surmang monastery, a five-day journey away, came to the area looking for the incarnation (*tulku* in Tibetan) of the tenth Trungpa Rinpoche, who had died in 1938. They took the names of one-year-old children from prominent families and left without visiting the nomads' tents. Only on their second visit did the Surmang monks make a thorough search and correctly identify the eleventh Trungpa.

Belief in karma and rebirth is widespread throughout Asia. The concept of intentional reincarnation is unusual among the Tibetans because buddhism explicitly repudiates the idea of a permanent, continuous self or soul that is reborn in successive lifetimes. However, Tibetan buddhists do believe in a momentum or continuity between lifetimes that is governed by one's level of spiritual attainment. The status and realm of rebirth is determined by one's karmic accumulation and is therefore involuntary. However, highly realized or enlightened beings who have transcended the cycle of birth and death (which buddhists call *samsara*) can *voluntarily* choose rebirth in the human realm in order to benefit other beings by their activity. The exact circumstances are conveyed to their followers so they can locate and train the next tulku. (The Tibetan tradition is the only buddhist tradition in the world that practices this unique form of succession.) The means of identifying tulkus are typically twofold: the lama either leaves a prediction letter before his death, or transmits the circumstances of his rebirth via a vision or dream to another realized teacher. This latter means is how Chögyam Trungpa was discovered.

In the eleventh Trungpa's case, the details of his rebirth appeared to the head of his lineage, the sixteenth Gyalwa Karmapa, in two successive visions. The first suggested that the village sounded like *Ge-De* and that the family had two children. The second was far more explicit, containing the exact names of the father and mother and the facts that the family lived in a tent that faced south and had a big red dog. These details of course corresponded to the infant Trungpa's family, although the Surmang monks were at first confused by the fact that the fathers' names did not match. Only on further questioning did they discover that the infant's natural father, who had left his mother during her pregnancy, had the exact name that the Karmapa had specified.

Trungpa Rinpoche's early life and training are beautifully described in his autobiography *Born in Tibet*, published in 1966. The world in which he grew up was medieval in its simplicity, without motor vehicles, electricity or telecommunications. The only wheeled artifact was the hand-held prayer wheel. Protected behind the Himalayas, Tibet had developed into a hermetic society distinguished by its isolation and cultural purity. But the volcanic forces of twentieth-century upheaval did not spare it. Ancient territorial claims by the Chinese resurfaced after civil war brought the communists to power in Beijing in 1949. Gradual colonization in the 1950s led to outright rebellion by the Tibetans in 1959 and a full-scale Chinese invasion. The Chinese communists were violently hostile toward Tibetan theocracy, which they believed kept the population in feudal servitude. They began to destroy monasteries, and imprison, torture and execute religious leaders. Trungpa Rinpoche, visiting his teacher in a nearby province, learned the Chinese were seeking to arrest him. He and a party of followers decided to flee to India. The description of their harrowing, nine-month trek across Tibet and into India forms the second half of Rinpoche's autobiography and is the subject of a fascinating documentary film, *Touch and Go*, made by one of Rinpoche's students. Many people died en route and the party was almost apprehended several times. By the end of the trip, survivors were reduced to boiling and eating their leather bags. Finally, in January 1960, their small party reached the Indian frontier. Trungpa Rinpoche was nineteen.

By many accounts, Chögyam Trungpa was an unusually brilliant scholar and teacher in a society distinguished by such attainment. In Northern India he was appointed to oversee the Young Lamas' Home School in Dalhousie by the Dalai Lama. But he was also already unconventional. Despite his monastic vows, he had an intimate relationship with a Tibetan nun who gave birth to a son in 1962 at Bodhgaya, the birthplace of the historical Buddha. (This individual is now Sakyong Mipham Rinpoche, spiritual head of the Shambhala community.) Having learned English in his youth, in 1963 he received a scholarship to study comparative religion at Oxford University, where he encountered Western spiritual seekers for the first time. He was to live in Britain for the next seven years, eventually becoming the first Tibetan British subject.

On his return from Bhutan in 1968, Rinpoche's period of uncertainty lasted several months through the ensuing winter. Then in May 1969, while driving in the city of Newcastle, he blacked out and crashed into a shop that sold jokes and novelties. When he recovered consciousness in the hospital, he learned that a blood clot in his brain had left him paralyzed on his left side. Though he would regain some motor function over time, he remained partially paralyzed for the rest of his life. It was as if the car accident were the unequivocal message that Rinpoche had been anticipating. He later explained that he understood its meaning was to underscore his deficit of compassion toward his Western students. He could not discard his Tibetan identity and credentials, but he could discard their trappings. Thus one of his first decisions upon beginning his recuperation was to disrobe and renounce his monastic vows.

This decision caused an outcry among both the Tibetan and Western residents at Samye Ling. In October 1969 he met Diana Pybus, a sixteen-year-old schoolgirl, and soon after proposed to her; they were married in Edinburgh on January 3, 1970. Relations at Samye Ling deteriorated rapidly after this. Many Western students were appalled by his conduct. Trungpa and his dharma brother Akong Rinpoche, with whom he had escaped from Tibet, lived in Oxford and founded Samye Ling, were no longer on speaking terms. After receiving an invitation to teach at the University of Colorado, Trungpa Rinpoche and Diana decided to leave for the United States. Without money, Diana had to petition Akong Rinpoche for the funds to buy airline tickets. Akong agreed to a loan, but kept the Trungpa seals and other precious artifacts that had been brought from Tibet as collateral. In March 1970, Trungpa Rinpoche and Diana left for Canada, never to reside in Britain again.

I accomplished the jailbreak from provincial Yorkshire in 1970 through steady performance on local and national examinations. Martin and I even won scholarships to Cambridge University, beyond our imaginings. My three years at Cambridge were largely agreeable—in no small measure because the formal requirements were so loose—although they did little to prepare me for the world of work I would encounter on leaving.

In the early Seventies, Cambridge University was rigidly segregated by gender and polarized by class. Roughly half the ten thousand undergraduates were students from state schools like Martin and me who had won places in open competition. The other half were from public schools, many of whom came to Cambridge on "closed" scholarships—reserved specifically for graduates of the most wealthy and influential schools. The two camps did not mix. The public school guys tended to favor sports like rugby and crew, wore blazers and cavalry twills and were known derisively as "hearties." We "grammar grubs" played soccer, drank beer and grew our hair long (I am oversimplifying a little). Besides these markers, the camps recognized each other instantly though voice accent—the grammar blokes speaking the florid array of regional British accents, the hearties the uniform slur of public school English in which "house" tends to rhyme with "mice." But mutual hostility became violent only rarely, and both camps were largely content with their separation. A far greater problem at Cambridge was the lack of women.

Men outnumbered women at the university by roughly eight to one, a cruel arithmetic that distorted all social relations. The difficulty of getting laid proved a dreadful obstacle and made many of us lonely and miserable. I managed to lose my virginity in my first term to a woman from London who worked as a civil servant, but my first year was largely solitary. I would sometimes attend musical or artistic events at one of the three women's colleges simply to be able to look at the opposite sex. Most of the guys I knew who were in relationships were with women from outside the university, either from their hometowns or from one of the language schools in the town. Consequently, I worked quite hard in my first year, even coming top in my college's end-of-year examinations and winning a coveted "First." It meant little at the time.

My loneliness and frustration abated in my second year. Through my interest in writing I met two guys at my college who ran the weekly arts magazine *Broadsheet*. John and Gordon were a year older than me, both Northern grammar school guys and English majors like me, who had big plans for overhauling the staid arts magazine. Gordon had a keen sense of design and was also intensely political—he was determined to recast the "feel" of the magazine and introduce a serious news section. John was a major culture vulture and was committed to making *Broadsheet* an in-depth, comprehensive guide to the Cambridge arts scene. To this end, they defied the paternalistic housing policy of the University and rented a dilapidated house a mile or so from the college. (At this time, the University required that all "junior members"—undergraduates—live in college or in "digs" with an approved landlady.) Their goal was to make their new pad the hub of magazine planning, design and production, and in their determination they actually pulled it off. In this era I would often marvel at their energy and creativity, riding around in the back of John's clapped-out Triumph Herald as he and Gordon interrupted each other with their plans and ideas. I, of course, wanted on board in the biggest way. By the end of that first term, I moved out of my college room and into their rented house and signed on as *Broadsheet*'s circulation manager.

There was a parallel, major development that winter in my romantic life—I met Tessa, a student at the teacher training college, who became my first serious lover. She was clever and mischievous, but also reserved and thoughtful. I was immediately smitten and suggested she accompany me back to my place the first night we met. She properly declined, and I quickly inferred that Tessa was a well-bred young woman who was not about to chuck herself at any guy she met on a Saturday night. But she agreed to see me again, and we began dating.

I was right about the breeding. Tessa's family lived in the stockbroker belt south of London and her father, a Cambridge graduate, was a corporate lawyer. Her mother was a homemaker who was active in her church. Tessa and her siblings attended public schools as day students, and Tessa herself had been the head prefect—quite a stretch from my own background (neither of my parents made it past tenth grade, were committed atheists and I was a notorious rebel as a schoolboy). But Tessa was neither spoiled nor snobbish and instead had a strain of otherness that made her very alluring. In particular, she had spent a year at an exclusive girls' prep school north of New York City, which furnished her with a cool inflection in her accent and a series of adventures that made my jaw drop; one had entailed a cross-country trip in a converted hearse with a traumatized Vietnam veteran.

A month or so into the relationship, Tessa greeted me after class with a tight hug and the whispered confession that she was ready to spend the night with me. It was a deep awakening for both of us, and I experienced an extended period of rapturous contentment. It also began a more active period of interest in the United States, because Tessa could now flesh out my curiosity with her experiences. At the end of my second year at Cambridge, my exam results came nowhere near the heights of year one—I was having way too much fun to apply myself to my studies.

When I began writing espionage fiction in the 1980s, I conceived my police detective hero Derek Smailes as an alter ego, a less neurotic version of myself. Smailes has a fascination with Americana, which makes him distrusted at the Cambridge police station. I wrote:

> The United States became a safety valve for his imagination, a place of deserts and forests and cities, of cornball decency and shocking excess, a place where things happened. He was particularly attracted to a certain kind of American renegade. He liked Jack Nicholson, who grew defiantly fat and bald as Redford and Hoffman ate grapefruit and pursued romantic lead roles. He liked Mailer, who threw punches on the cusp of journalism and literature. And he liked Willie Nelson, above all, who reminded him of the country singers he had listened to on the PX jukebox as a boy.

Apart from Willie Nelson, who has always left me cold, I was writing about my young self. During my long exile in the United States, I have gradually come to see British culture through its distorting lens, and I understand how Americans tend to see the British as the epitome of class, in its sense of polish, sophistication and wit—the Masterpiece Theater syndrome. But for a young man in Britain who was alert to cultural messages in the 1960s, there was really no contest. Herman's Hermits were not the Jefferson Airplane, Donovan Leitch was not Bob Dylan, and Philip Larkin was not Allen Ginsberg. The cultural heavy hitters were all American, perhaps in some large measure because the United States had initiated the defining event of the era, the Vietnam War, which all these icons resisted in their own unique and astonishing ways. We had Swinging London and the Mersey Beat, but America had tate, the Siege of Chicago and Woodstock. We looked across the Atlantic with awe, and many of us resolved to experience American culture directly. Thus I was enthralled when Tessa would recount tales of visiting the homes of her wealthy school friends, the twenty-four hour supermarkets and swimming pool parties. But she'd also encountered a rawer reality, attending anti-war rallies and meeting veterans. It was a connection I envied and wanted to emulate.

My third and final year at Cambridge was more difficult. Unintentionally, I had put myself in line to take over *Broadsheet*, because circulation manager was the traditional grunt position that was rewarded the following year with the editorship. My problem was that I was content being a grunt. I always felt like a spear-carrier around John and Gordon, who were brilliant individually but in tandem were unstoppable. I had no similar ally on whom to call, and no particular vision for the magazine beyond wanting to extend what they had accomplished. But the alternatives were stark: either hand the magazine over to someone untried, or allow the magazine to fold. My sense of duty prevailed, and I accepted the reins of the magazine, along with another guy from Sidney Sussex College, a clever but elusive writer for Gordon's column whom none of us knew well.

Editing *Broadsheet* did not sit particularly well with me. I found the responsibility and the four-day production schedule onerous. I could do no academic work and was exhausted all the time. Worse, I hated the sense that I might have become a "Cambridge personality" and found myself unwilling to display gestures like holding hands with Tessa in public, which I deemed uncool and therefore to be avoided. I dreaded showing up in the gossip column of one of the rival publications, which thankfully never happened. I wanted to carry a spear again, not occupy center stage, and eventually made my excuses to my co-editor about needing to get a degree, and quit after one term.

Tensions developed with Tessa also. By now we were spending almost every night together and the relationship became claustrophobic. My greatest aspiration was to be cool, and I felt that together we were not—we were too immature, too dependent. If I had a reservation about Tessa, it was that she was *too* well-bred, that she ought to stand up for herself more. For her part, I knew she often found my social milieu obnoxious and intimidating; we were loud and opinionated and she was too often a silent nonparticipant among us. Things came to a head one night after I'd spent time with some university women we both knew. She said quietly that she was afraid she held me back, that I would find more freedom outside the relationship. I confessed that I felt this too. The choice seemed inevitable, and we stayed awake in dread the rest of the night. As it got light, she asked quietly, Are you just gonna' go? and I did.

I was a wreck for days and we agreed to meet to talk. We almost immediately fell into bed again with relief and embarrassment—despite our dissatisfaction with the relationship, neither of us could break away yet. That would take several more years. I did manage to get a degree…just. I buckled down after Christmas and caught up the bare minimum to pass my exams. I was relieved when the final year at Cambridge was over, although equivocal about what lay ahead of me.

One big problem with my education is that it ended so abruptly without any preparation for what came next. I had worked during vacations in both high school and college, but had hardly accrued any job skills. And my experience as an English major had hardly inculcated much of a work ethic—all I had to do was show up for a one-hour academic supervision per week, and that was it. And because that paper trail was easy to fake, it was possible to spend a whole term at Cambridge and not even open a book, as I did when I edited *Broadsheet*. Americans don't get it—You didn't go to class? they ask. There were no classes, only an array of lectures that was optional and widely ignored. So we could easily get up at eleven and fix breakfast in our rooms as we fired up the day's first joint. No wonder we were unprepared for what came next.

Somebody I ran into during my final year told me he was applying for jobs in journalism because "it didn't close any doors." This made sense to me, and I resolved to do the same. The one thing I knew about myself was that I liked to write, and that was what journalists did, I reasoned. After all, I had to do something, so I applied to the newspaper groups that had training programs for graduates like me. I was hired by the Thomson Group (Lord Thomson of Fleet, the guy who invented the *Yellow Pages*, was a Canadian-born British media baron). Thomson owned a stable of provincial newspapers, in addition to *The Times* and *The Sunday Times* of London. Out of the blue I was told that I had been assigned to the *Belfast Evening Telegraph*, the national newspaper of Northern Ireland.

Any doubts I had about my choice evaporated. It was surely destiny—I would go to war-torn Belfast and establish myself as an intrepid chronicler of sectarian conflict. At my interview in the *Telegraph*'s newsroom I met my future editors, doughty newsmen in shirtsleeves and suspenders who smoked unfiltered cigarettes in glass-paneled offices as typewriters clattered in thebackground. It seemed almost—cool. But first I had to complete a three-month training course in South Wales.

The program in Cardiff was run by a couple of clapped-out news hacks who thought we were a bunch of snot-nosed brats who did not know the first thing about their craft. Fair enough, we didn't. We began an intensive course in newspaper law, shorthand and simulated exercises in which we would file putative "stories" from the field to our "newsrooms." It was all useful stuff. I bonded quickly with a couple of guys—Richard, a lanky, elegant fellow with newsprint in his blood (his uncle was an editor in Newcastle) and Malcolm, a small, dashing and endearing man who had graduated, by coincidence, from Queen's University in Belfast the previous year. Richard and Malcolm shared the connection that they had both lost their fathers in their teens. Malcolm and I shared the connection that we were both in unresolved, long-term relationships with women from the university. Tessa had graduated with me and was now working in a daycare center in South London. Malcolm's girlfriend was finishing up her last year in Belfast. Malcolm, Richard and I took a seedy flat together near the city center and our friendship did a lot to offset the chill wind of reality that was blowing through our lives.

For my part, a sense of foreboding only grew stronger as the course progressed and my transfer to Belfast grew steadily closer. I could fulfill the requirements of the course quite handily and fancied myself an able reporter, but the truth was (which I sensed was obvious to my superiors) that my heart wasn't in it. Occasionally I got to write some Orwellian piece about conditions in the coal mines, but largely I was dispirited. The profession of journalism seemed to me a cynical and reductive enterprise to which I was ill-suited. Furthermore, I was now reading the *Belfast Telegraph* daily and developing a strong sense of how dreadful things were over there. In addition to the organized campaign of IRA bombings against commercial and government targets, a wave of tit-for-tat sectarian killings had broken out, targeting ordinary citizens. At home, matters between Tessa and me were in limbo. I was assigned to Belfast for two years, and there was no sense that she would accompany me over there. But how could we sustain our relationship at such a distance? She visited me in Cardiff a couple of times; our reunions were tender but clouded by these unanswered questions. My sense of impending doom was palpable when I stayed with her in London before heading out to Northern Ireland. One night we came home and I sat on her bed and began shaking uncontrollably. She put her arms round me and said, *You need tranks, mate.* But I was yet to fill my first tranquilizer prescription, and headed off to Belfast fortified by nothing other than my own shaky resolve.

three

The city of Belfast was a dour Victorian place not unlike Glasgow, a place I knew well. But whereas Glasgow's rough edges were softened by the warmth and humor of its people, Belfast was a city under military siege, and its mood was tense and grim. The Troubles (the quaint term the locals used for the sectarian violence between Protestants and Catholics) had begun, or rather resumed, in the summer of 1969 following a modest civil rights campaign modeled on the example set by Dr. King in the United States. The demonstrators were nearly all Catholics, protesting the systemic abuse of power by the Protestant-dominated provincial government. In early 1969, nonviolent marchers found themselves under attack by Protestant gangs, as the local police, the Royal Ulster Constabulary, stood by. The Catholic population began to mobilize to protect itself, and sectarian violence erupted into open warfare in August 1969 during a three-day riot known as The Battle of Bogside, named for the Catholic neighborhood in Derry, Ulster's second-largest city. After the Irish Prime Minister threatened to send troops to protect Catholics, British Prime Minister Harold Wilson sent in the British army to restore order. The soldiers were initially welcomed by the Catholic population, who hated and feared the local police.

The tormented history of England and Ireland spans some 800 years, a ghastly chronicle of greed, violence and treachery. I knew very little of it when I showed up in Belfast with my cardboard suitcase and cheap overcoat in January 1974, but I quickly understood the broad outline. Ulster, the northernmost of the six Irish provinces, had a population of some 1.5 million, two-thirds of whom were Protestant. (The population of the rest of Ireland is 98 percent Catholic.) This Protestant majority existed because of the Ulster Plantation of the early seventeenth century. Similar to the Virginia Plantation at Jamestown, its goal was for British settlers to pacify the indigenous population and commercially exploit the region for the British crown. Ulster was chosen because historically it was the most Gaelic, and the most rebellious province of the restive Irish colony. Because James I of England was also James VI of Scotland and the two kingdoms were now unified, it was agreed that half the Ulster settlers would be Scots. Although the settlement did not succeed quite as planned (the goal had been to extirpate *all* Catholics), English Anglicans and Scots Presbyterians became the majority, land-owning class in Ulster by the late 1600s, and remained so into the twentieth century. When the Irish Free State (the precursor of the Republic of Ireland) was granted independence from the British crown in 1920, Northern Ireland with its Protestant majority was partitioned to remain part of the United Kingdom. The modern conflict in Northern Ireland has been between *republicans* (Catholics who want reunification with the Irish Republic) and *unionists* or *loyalists* (Protestants who want the province to remain part of the United Kingdom).

What was bizarre for me from the start in Belfast was that everyone in the province looked the same—they were white Europeans like me who spoke with the same strange accent in which "now" sounded like "nigh." But ordinary Ulster folk seemed to know each other's ethnic identity *instantly*, and they hated and feared each other with Pleistocene savagery. Nothing had prepared me for this. The hearties and the grubs at Cambridge might throw insults and the occasional punch at each other—in Ulster, militia members would routinely execute their enemies in front of their wives and children. And by the time I got there in 1974, the paramilitaries, far more than the British army, were calling the shots. The most feared and violent of these was the Provisional Irish Republican Army, known as the Provos.

The Provos had broken away from the Official IRA during the recrimination that followed the attacks on Catholics in 1969. Founded in 1919 during the War of Independence that overthrew British rule, the IRA was taunted by some Bogside residents during the riots that summer by their declaring that the initials stood for "I Ran Away." In truth, the IRA had scant organization or weaponry during the siege of the Bogside, but in the aftermath its leadership did oppose the calls for outright war against the British occupation from some of its members. These men broke away to form the Provisionals, who, jump-started by cash from Dublin, began to organize for guerrilla warfare against the British. Their ultimate goal was to overthrow *both* the governments in the north and south and establish a unified socialist republic of Ireland. When I got to Belfast, this campaign manifested mainly as attacks on property, on British soldiers and on members of the Protestant paramilitary groups that had sprung up to oppose them.

The weapon of choice was the homemade bomb. The IRA never employed suicide tactics (self-inflicted fatalities were mistakes known as "own goals"), so the bombs were planted in bags, suitcases or, frequently, vehicles, and left to detonate with timing devices. Sometimes coded warnings were phoned in, minimizing casualties; sometimes they were not. Sometimes the bombs were found and defused by army experts; often they were not. After David and I found our own flat, we would play a game each evening in which we would listen to the bombs detonating around Belfast between six and nine p.m., then try and guess their size (a three-pounder sounded and felt a lot different from a twenty-five-pounder—a twenty-five pounder you felt through your feet.) Then we would turn on the evening news to see how close our guesses had been, knowing we might be covering the follow-up story the next day.

David and I were the two English trainees from the Cardiff program destined for the Belfast newsroom. David was an unusual guy. At twenty-three, he looked and acted like a much older person. Balding and slightly stooped, he was a dedicated member of the British Labour Party, and had even been chosen to stand for Parliament at the next election in a die-hard Conservative district. Whereas most of the guys in Cardiff (at least Malcolm and I) were still largely concerned with the football results and sex, David was concerned with West Bank relations and regional development policy. But despite lifestyle discrepancies, David and I had a high regard for each other and there was never any doubt that we would get a flat together. We quickly found an elegant place out on the Malone Road at a modest rent—there was not a lot of demand for rental property in Belfast in this era.

A note on Belfast geography: the city map is like a spider. An inner ring of concentric streets forms the "body" or city center, from which major roads branch out like "legs." Most of these became household names in Britain for their association with ethnic neighborhoods—the Falls Road to the Southwest, leading to Andersonstown and the Catholic neighborhoods; the Shankill to the West and Ormeau Roads to the Southeast leading to the Protestant areas. Further South were the Malone and Lisburn Roads that led to the middle-class enclaves that were supposedly nonsectarian. This statement discloses a basic truth about the Troubles—they were fundamentally a working-class conflict, which is one reason the Provos' revolutionary utopianism was so misguided; the Protestant worker hated and feared the pope vastly more than his capitalist oppressor. Naturally, David and I chose a "safe" middle-class neighborhood in which to live; the Malone Road was never the site of car bombs since there were no identifiable targets there.

My nerves steadied somewhat as I adjusted to life as a cub reporter. David and I were assigned the bottom tier of news stories—diamond anniversaries, complaints about poor bus service and the like. But inevitably, as Northern Ireland's newspaper of record, the *Telegraph* dealt daily with the civil and sectarian conflicts raging in the city, and everyone on the staff was drawn into it. I quickly found myself in improbable situations: interviewing a drunk who staggered into the newsroom because he had "ratted" on his son for joining the UDA, the main Protestant guerrilla army, and feared assassination; visiting Long Kesh, a bona fide concentration camp where the British government interned republican prisoners behind chain link, barbed wire and watchtowers; attending a rally to protest the force-feeding of Dolours and Marian Price, a famous pair of IRA sisters who, in 1973, had been convicted of a car bombing outside the Old Bailey, London's high court, and were now on hunger strike in a British prison.

This last event handily illustrates the gulf I had to cross to perform my job in Belfast. The rally, held in front of the Divis Flats, a grim Catholic housing project near the city center, was led by Maire Drumm, a fiery orator and scion of a famous republican clan. Standing on the back of a flatbed truck, Drumm inflamed the crowd through a bullhorn with a speech about the inhumanity of the Price sisters' treatment. Her fury was palpable, and the crowd howled its indignation as she vilified the British government and denounced the army snipers stationed on surrounding rooftops. Closer at hand, other soldiers stood near their Saracen armored cars holding rifles. Drumm then demonstrated the force-feeding procedure, leaning back in a chair as a leather funnel was shoved into her gullet. Pushing it away violently, she vomited over the front ranks of the crowd before picking up the bullhorn again and raving further. The crowd screamed back. Needless to say, I had never seen anything like this, and was unsure how to write about it. But I must have written something that the news desk could use, because a story and accompanying picture appeared the next day. (As a coda, Maire Drumm was assassinated in 1976 in a Belfast hospital while recovering from eye surgery. Loyalist paramilitaries dressed as doctors burst in and shot her.)

Soon after, even this minimal response failed me. Because I was a rookie, I pulled the unpopular Saturday shift. Saturday was a notoriously slow news day, and there was usually little to do before repairing to McGlades, the journalists' bar next door, at around five. Around four, the news editor hailed me and told me to check out the report of a "wee fire" at a sports shop a few blocks away. See if you can file something for a box, he said. (By four p.m., the paper had already "gone to bed" and was being printed. However, in the days of hot-metal type, the presses could be stopped and late copy slugged into a box on the front page that was called the "Stop Press" box. It was a handy sales gimmick for the hawkers on the sidewalk.) I walked over to the site of the fire and soon realized there was nothing "wee" about it. The police had cordoned off the entire block and were holding back big crowds at both ends, and there were a good twenty fire trucks present. Just like in the movies, I showed my press pass and pushed past the barrier. The scene made my jaw drop. The "sports shop" was a major sports department store seven stories high that was completely engulfed in flames that shot fifty feet into the evening sky. Firemen on ladders trained plumes of water into the inferno. In the camping department on the fifth floor, canisters of propane exploded like bombs, blowing out glass onto the street. I was frozen in awe until I remembered I was supposed to file a "box." I found a pay phone and dialed the copy line. (In this era, reporters called in their stories from the field to "copy girls," women who sat at manual typewriters with headsets.)

Okay, said the copy girl when I got through.

Box, I said, giving her the slug line. There's an enormous fucking fire....

I beg your pardon, said the typist in her wonderful Ulster brogue.

Oh Jesus. There's a fire, I said again. I was in shock, unable to remember the first thing about how to construct a news story.

I felt a hand on my shoulder spin me around and then grab the receiver. It was John, an experienced reporter whom the news editor had sent over as soon as he realized the scale of the "wee fire." I stood by in awe as my colleague filed a completely fluent three-paragraph account from a series of shorthand squiggles. Humbled, I doubted whether I would ever be able to muster the detachment to function like that under pressure. Everything was so new to me, so intense.

Personally I was exquisitely lonely in Belfast. David and I were cordial, not intimately friendly. A friend of Martin's from Cambridge who had moved back to Belfast after graduating took me out occasionally to cheer me up. But quickly I became dependent on Malcolm's girlfriend Jean for companionship and commiseration. Jean was (somewhat predictably, since Malcolm was a man of impeccable taste) quite beautiful. She was also hysterically unhappy about her separation from Malcolm and the long-term prospects for their relationship. We quickly established a close rapport. Occasionally we would go to a movie, but mostly we sat in the pub for hours, chatting gloomily. We both needed to talk, and found in the other an eager listener. I was always ready for a few pints in the evening to steady myself (so I reasoned), but Jean tended to favor the local winter brew of hot whisky (Scotch, with lemon juice, sugar and boiling water). One Friday night she got especially hammered and asked that I help her get home. Once back at her room we began making out, and an alarm bell went off.

This is not a good idea, I said, stopping.

I suppose not, said Jean. Don't go.

So I didn't, crossing a bridge to a place I'd never been before. Thus Jean and I began a deeply unhappy affair.

My last few weeks in Belfast are somewhat a blur to me. Tormented by guilt, I stopped sleeping, dragging myself into work each day like a zombie. I could not stop seeing Jean since she was the only human contact I had in Belfast, but I could not avoid the new sexual nature of our relationship. We tried to ignore it—which did not work. But she was not my girlfriend—she was my new friend Malcolm's girlfriend. It was an unspeakable position. I began to feel worse than I had ever felt in my life.

Around this time the coalition government of Conservative Prime Minister Edward Heath collapsed, and he was forced to call a general election. By law in Britain the general election campaign lasts just three weeks. David immediately applied for and was granted leave to contest his parliamentary seat in Yorkshire; I was left alone in our Belfast flat. I began to feel increasingly shaky both at work and at home. In one particularly awful week, I interviewed the manager of a petrol station about the effect on his business of a recent price hike. The man happened to be Catholic. The evening after the story appeared I watched the news and saw that the same man had been assassinated on his doorstep later that same day. Cruelly, I was dispatched the following morning to do the "follow-up" with the man's widow. The bloodstains were still fresh at our feet as I spoke with her. As I was obliged to, I asked the woman whether her husband was a member of any "banned organizations." The question was deeply insulting. She angrily denied the suggestion, and I felt a deep sense of disgust at my intrusion into her grief.

On another occasion, the news editor told me to sign out a car and check on a story brewing in the Ardoyne, a Catholic neighborhood badly damaged during the '69 riots. The housing authority had refurbished a street of burned-out row houses and, as a reconciliation gesture, planned to install homeless families from both the Protestant and Catholic communities. The paper had received a tip that the IRA was planning to jump the gun and install only republican families. I found the street, a dead end in a bleak modern housing estate. It was mid-afternoon and the street seemed deserted. Taking the precaution of turning the car around first, I parked and got out. I saw that a man in a leather jacket stood watching me from the front window of a vacant house, his right hand inside the zipper at his armpit. He disappeared and then the front door opened and he advanced toward me, his hand still at his armpit. I turned and walked away quickly, got in the car and drove off, my heart pumping wildly.

Realistically, by now my days were numbered in Belfast—my emotional reserves were exhausted, and it was simply a matter of time before I could no longer function in such an environment. The interval might have been longer however, had I not run into Kevin Wiggins again. Wiggins was a truly bizarre person, an Englishman and former British soldier who told me when we met that he had come to Belfast to join the RUC, the Royal Ulster Constabulary. Soldiers becoming policemen was not uncommon; a former British soldier planning to join the all-Irish Protestant RUC was really strange. Various things about Wiggins didn't fit. He was tall, ungainly and conservatively dressed, but spoke a peculiar hippie argot. He claimed to have a wife and children in North Wales, but here he was trying to move to Ulster and enlist in the RUC. I thought at the time—and still think—that he might have been working for army intelligence. I had not seen him for weeks when we ran into each other again. He invited me over to his neighborhood for a drink on Saturday night; he'd moved into a room in a house off the Ormeau Road. David had left and I was trying to avoid Jean, so I accepted.

Wiggins and I sat in his local pub talking about God knows what. At some point he went into his wallet, pulled out a couple of purple tablets and asked me if I wanted to drop acid. Now during my student years I had been a fairly enthusiastic consumer of beer and pot. Hallucinogens intimidated me, however, and I had only taken them a few times in very controlled circumstances. My judgment that night was really poor. Feeling I had nothing to lose, I swilled the tab down with a swallow of beer. By the time the drug began to come on the pub was closing, so we headed back to Wiggins' room.

During my time in Belfast I was a foot soldier—riding the bus or walking, because I was way too poor to afford a car or taxis. I'd thus planned to crash on Wiggins' floor, until it turned out he had no bedding and suggested instead we share his double bed together. I felt a wave of paranoia. Was Wiggins gay? Were the drugs and the alcohol just a ruse just to get me in the sack? Truly he was weird enough for *anything* to be true. I declined forcefully and said I'd walk home. He seemed embarrassed and said he'd take the floor if I wanted the bed. By now I needed out of there in the worst way, so I made my apologies and left. As I stepped outdoors I realized I was tripping fairly hard and now faced the task of walking home across Belfast after midnight. I thought I knew the geography well enough—west to the Lagan River, then southwest up to the Malone Road. I tried not to think of the Lagan's reputation as a dumping ground for bodies as I set out—painfully slowly it felt, my feet a long way away.

After a journey of what seemed like several hours but which was probably only twenty minutes, I walked down a steep street and could see the Lagan at the bottom. The streets were deserted. At the bottom of the hill was a fiercely illuminated police station, which like all Belfast police stations was fortified like a military command post. Vicious speed bumps and concrete bollards discouraged car bombers; a sandbagged machine gun bunker to the side of the main doors protected the entrance. I could see the glint of the sentry's gun barrel as he picked up my movement as I approached. The barrel followed me as I passed slowly in front of the station. What the hell would I say if I was challenged? I'm just on my way home because an ex-soldier on acid just tried to seduce me? There was no verbal challenge, but the barrel did not leave its target as I passed in front of the station, crossed a bridge and walked along the far side of the river. I was aware that I was breathing heavily and that the sweat was beading on my forehead.

I will never know the explanation for what happened next. Maybe they were bad guys, maybe they weren't. Maybe they were just lost, although I doubt it. A car passed me then stopped fifteen yards ahead. There was no traffic or pedestrians around. The road was dark. Slowly, the passenger's side window was wound down. There was no point running, nor was there any point pretending I hadn't noticed the car or that it was waiting for me. This could be it, I remember thinking. This is how you die. I reached the car and bent down to speak to the passenger. He looked up at me, then turned sharply and spoke to the driver. Then the car sped away, the window winding up.

The next day something had snapped; the acid trip had shattered whatever reserves I had left. I must have looked awful because I remember borrowing milk from a neighbor and seeing her look at me in terror. The thought of going into work the next day was impossible. The prospect of quitting, returning to London and telling Malcolm and Tessa what I had done was worse. I went out to buy cigarettes—Park Drive was my brand, an evil little unfiltered number with a big kick. Trying to strike a match, the box slipped from my hand and the matches cascaded in a bloom to the sidewalk. Even simple tasks were beyond me. I returned to the flat. It was cold. I looked at the gas fire and thought about turning on the burner, and not lighting it. That would solve the problem. Then I found the phone book and called the Samaritans, the crisis intervention group for desperate, suicidal people like me.

I do not remember the plane trip from Belfast to London, or how I got from the airport to my sister's house in Islington. In her living room I remember feeling physically safe at last, but very frightened that I would have to be hospitalized. I do not remember whether or not I called Jean to tell her I was leaving, but I do remember calling both Tessa and Malcolm and telling them I needed to talk to them both.

four

My memories of this first real experience of major depression in the spring of 1974 remain quite vivid. Others have written about this experience most eloquently, and I am loath to try to emulate their achievement at great length. Starting with William Styron's harrowing, pellucid *Darkness Visible* in 1990, a succession of writers (I single out David Foster Wallace's short story "The Depressed Person" [1999] and Donald Hall's essay "The Ghost in the House" [2002]) has described the peculiar horror of this misunderstood affliction in ways that serve to demystify it. Styron in particular deserves credit for jump-starting the phenomenon of the celebrity depressive prepared to bare his or her soul in public. Such candor has served to diminish the stigma associated with the disorder, which is still one of its most distressing aspects for sufferers.

The terminology I used myself once I was safe in London was that I had "cracked up," or suffered a "nervous breakdown." Neither term is sufficiently clinical to win favor with the medical establishment, but each handily conveys something of the excruciating reality of this state. I once met a lecturer from West Point whose specialty was the chilling field of human engineering. He described the effects on Iraqi officers during the first Gulf War when the U.S. command, having broken Iraqi codes, was able to anticipate and respond to orders from Baghdad before they were even received by the Iraqis. The Iraqi response to such helplessness was either paralysis or palsy, he calmly explained, which struck an immediate chord with me—this was my own response to the helplessness of depression. Even the smallest daily tasks of dressing, bathing and eating became arduous. More complicated ones that required concentration, like reading, entailed huge effort. Complex tasks were simply out. During this most severe phase, time is cruelly distorted and all sense of perspective is lost. The minutes and hours crawl past in a malign inversion of the "time flies" bromide. Ordinary phenomena become menacing and sinister. I remember watching the general election returns in which the Labour Party won a tiny majority (my colleague David, of course, lost in a landslide) and being appalled by the venom and malice of the politicians. Traveling on the London Underground was to encounter hordes of anonymous, malevolent people trapped in a deafening chamber rocketing through the void. I did not go out much, except to meet with my psychiatrist. I asked him anxiously what was likely to happen to me (I had gotten over the initial terror of hospitalization), and he told me breezily I was likely to suffer a depressive illness. No big deal, I thought—I'd experienced depression before. But as William Styron points out, we have but the one word to describe the ordinary mood fluctuation and the extraordinary, pathological version. This was the latter kind, and it was to prove a big deal.

Another big deal was my obligation to explain to Malcolm and to Tessa what had happened in Belfast. It never crossed my mind to dissimulate, although my prostrate condition handily forestalled the reactions of righteous anger that I knew I deserved, particularly from Malcolm. He had obviously spoken to Jean, and they had begun their own damage-control exercise. As it turned out, their relationship survived my malign intervention for several more years, and my friendship with Malcolm continued until his untimely death from cancer in the '90s; he never confided the level of private betrayal he likely felt.

As for Tessa, she was such a magnanimous person that she buried whatever hurt I had caused and welcomed me back into her life without recrimination. My long-suffering sister and her remarkably kind husband, who housed me during this period, were also very supportive. After about two weeks, when the most severe symptoms abated, I moved in with Tessa into the rambling house in South London whose tiny bathroom and kitchen she shared with about a dozen roommates. The task of recovery would take almost six months.

In 1974, the only anti-depressant medication available was slow acting and came with a host of side effects, so I tore up the prescription my psychiatrist insisted I take; the one for Valium I filled immediately. Thus began long days with little to do other than wander around London and delay as long as possible the ingestion of my daily dose of tranquilizers. Thomson Newspapers graciously offered me indefinite leave, inviting me to be back in touch when I felt ready to be reassigned. I had no clue when this might be, or whether indeed I might be finished with the newspaper business for good.

A pleasing chaos reigned in Tessa's house that provided some diversion. About half the residents were friends I knew from Cambridge, the rest an international cast of itinerants. Because of the absurd bathroom set-up there was no possibility of privacy; there were always at least one and sometimes up to four people using the place at the same time. The house was divided on whether Aidan, a yoga teacher, should be allowed to defecate from a squatting position atop the porcelain bowl when someone else was in the bathtub—an explosive performance that he insisted was both natural and healthy. The most vocal opponent of this practice was Muffy Hiss, our most exotic resident. Muffy was related to Alger Hiss, of Whittaker Chambers/Richard Nixon fame, and had come to London to be analyzed by Anna Freud, daughter of Sigmund. No doubt this analysis was sorely needed, because the blond, curvaceous Ms. Hiss had a strange penchant for the Older Man, and was dating an American guy who was considerably older than my dad. Muffy complained loudly about the old chap's insistence on frequent blowjobs, which she administered on a strict "quid pro blow" understanding of unlimited spending money. She was Tessa's neighbor in the cold, damp basement and like me, did not work. Occasionally we would hang out together, and she would recount stories of her debauched youth, in which stoned Florida teenagers drove sports cars into swimming pools for kicks. We came from different planets.

My days crawled by. Sometimes I would visit a museum or a gallery, but I had developed a queasy agoraphobia that could kick in anytime and send me scurrying home for the Valium bottle. My psychiatrist seemed discouraged that I was making little progress and made grave pronouncements about "emancipation problems." He thought it was unwise that I was living with Tessa but I could see no alternative. Tessa worked full-time at the daycare center and would return at six or so, exhausted and smelling of toddlers, to find her bored, neurotic and importunate boyfriend needing attention. Somehow she remained patient and supportive, which in hindsight amazes me.

One development in May provided a bizarre coda to my Belfast experience. We were spending the weekend at Tessa's parents' home in Surrey, an ample, comfortable place that was sharply in contrast to the teeming warren we inhabited in South London. Watching the Friday evening news, my attention was grabbed by the lead story from Northern Ireland about a raid that day on the IRA Belfast brigade headquarters that had captured its commander, the notorious republican fugitive Brendan Hughes. It was a big coup for the security forces and also suggested they had informants in high places, because the bust was in an unlikely, upscale neighborhood off the Malone Road. A shot of the "mansion" where Hughes had been arrested looked spookily familiar, and I reached for the phone and called David in Belfast. He answered on the first ring.

David, it's Tony, I said. Where was that IRA bust today?

Downstairs, he responded, in a shaky voice.

I listened in disbelief as he described coming home from work to find armed police surrounding the house and waiting for him in our flat. He had just returned from several hours' interrogation at the hands of the police. It turned out the ground floor of the building was a storage dump for gelignite, the IRA's preferred explosive. Directly below our apartment was a bomb factory—we had suspected nothing. David was clearly rattled but relieved his interrogation was over. His relief turned out to be premature. I called him a couple of times that weekend and got no answer, eventually reaching him again on Monday. He sounded very shaky, and he was making his own plans to leave Belfast. The story he told me was sobering.

David had gone to bed on Friday evening feeling that he had cleared up the question of any complicity on his part in the activities in the flat downstairs. That night, however, men armed with automatic weapons burst into the flat and hauled him away for further interrogation. They claimed to be army intelligence but wore no uniforms and would not identify themselves further. David, a scholar of the Ulster troubles, had copious left-wing literature in the flat relating to the Irish Question. The police must have passed this material on to the army who suspected that David was a fellow traveler if not an active supporter of the IRA. He was held incommunicado all weekend, and when he failed to show up for work on Monday, alarm bells went off in the *Telegraph* newsroom. The editor managed to locate him and secure his release, and followed up with an angry protest about the violation of press neutrality that David's arrest represented. David himself had been traumatized by the experience, and I worried that he was on the verge of his own breakdown. Within a month he had transferred to a paper in South Wales and the experiment of recruiting English trainees to the Belfast newsroom came to an end.

Spring became summer and I felt little improvement in my mood. I was increasingly haunted by the so-called "emancipation problems" my psychiatrist had identified, and felt they now likely extended to an un healthy dependence on Tessa. Although it felt premature, I contacted Thomson's personnel officer and told him I was ready for reassignment. I told him I preferred Edinburgh or Newcastle—I reasoned that I should move as far away as possible to prove I could strike out on my own again. As it turned out, only the editor of a newly launched paper in suburban London was interested to meet me. I traveled dejectedly to Hemel Hempstead, a postwar "new town," to meet the editor of the *Evening Echo* at its production plant on a bleak industrial estate and felt little gratification when I was offered the job. The only consolation was that Richard, my other flat mate from Cardiff, was already assigned to the paper. I had dismissed the notion of changing course; the Belfast debacle was the first time I had tried and failed at anything in my life and I had to prove that I could do this damn job, whether or not it ultimately meant anything to me.

Tessa likely felt a range of emotions when I moved out, but one of them must have been relief—the situation in her house was pretty untenable. I say "likely" because Tessa and I never developed the capacity to seriously discuss our relationship—an ultimately fatal deficit. Way too much between us was left unsaid. Thus our relationship resumed its unsatisfactory, tidal rhythm: not together, not apart. Soon we both found new places to live. Slowly but steadily, my confidence returned as I proved myself equal to the tasks the *Evening Echo* newsroom set me; it was a trashy paper that favored a jazzy style that was easy to write. I breathed a huge, inner sigh of relief that my Belfast experience seemed not to have left me permanently disabled.

That winter Tessa told me she was planning to take an extended trip back to Canada and the States—maybe three to six months—with her best friend Brenda. She had contacts in Ontario, Colorado and New Mexico. We both knew it was a gambit in our relationship—maybe time apart would tell us what we needed to know. She came up to spend a final weekend with me and there was both anticipation and somberness about our time together. I was sad but also eager for her to go. I watched her train head down its track to London until it was out of sight, then turned for home with that spring in the step that is distinctive to newly single men.

By the time Tessa had been gone a year I knew I was done with journalism—working on the *Evening Echo* had taught me that while I may be a competent journalist, newspapers would never be my vocation. My favorite description of the requirements for success in the profession came from the intrepid *Sunday Times* reporter Nicholas Tomalin, who was killed by a rocket strike on his car while reporting from the Golan Heights in 1973. "A rat-like cunning, a plausible manner, and a little literary ability" was his famous catalog. To these I would add tenacity—the determination to get the story at all costs—and it was in this area that I was most deficient. I would often be horrified by people's craven willingness to share the most personal details in order to get their names in the paper. I would find myself thinking, I'm going to ask you some really intrusive questions, but please have the dignity not to answer, and be secretly gratified if they did not. Needless to say, I was not the news editor's first choice when a big story had to be covered on a tight deadline.

I did satisfy myself that I was up to the job, and met the range of requirements of my two-year internship—reporting, copyediting, feature writing, staffing a satellite office. I spent many days in court and at local government meetings, eventually winning a promotion in my second year as education reporter. With the modest raise I bought myself a fast Japanese motorcycle—I was not about to capitulate to the suburban lifestyle just yet. I had flings with a couple of women I'd known at Cambridge, then a steadier relationship with a local girl. Emotionally, however, I remained celibate. For better or worse, Tessa still ruled my heart, and I wondered what would happen when we next saw each other.

When that would be became less and less clear. We stayed in touch by letter, and her trip had been stimulating but largely uneventful until she and Brenda traveled to New Mexico in the summer of 1975. Their destination was a loose hippie community they knew of—dozens of households in close proximity midway between Taos and Santa Fe. It wasn't quite a commune, since there was no charismatic leader, but the community was a full-blown expression of the Seventies counterculture and Tess and Bren, well-bred English girls both, took to the place like ducks to water. Tessa's letters began to fill with hedonistic tales of drugs, hot springs and topless gardening. And there were plenty of guys. Tessa was quite candid about which hippies they were with at any given point, guys with *noms de guerre* like Tado, Lem and Antler. I found the tales enthralling, because I could sense she was experiencing the soul expansion she had gone to the States to find. If I felt twinges of jealousy, it was largely because my own life was so humdrum. After several nomadic weeks, Tessa settled on the small ranch of Todd, the original hippie contact, and his rich wife Celeste. She would work on their land in return for room and board, and was learning to make jewelry. By the end of the summer Tessa wrote that she had decided to overstay her visa and remain indefinitely in New Mexico. Todd was a minister in some obscure church and was planning to marry her to one of the ranch hands so she could get her papers. This last development gave me pause.

During the first winter that Tessa was in New Mexico in 1975, I did finally make a three-hundred-mile motorcycle trip to Samye-Ling, the Tibetan buddhist meditation center in Scotland, seven years after I first heard of the place. As part of my recovery in South London, I'd begun taking yoga classes with my housemate Aidan, the acrobatic defecator. I was not particularly adept at the different *asanas* he taught us, but I was drawn to the periods of meditation at the end of each session—they offered a real sense of peace, an inkling that I might someday be well again. I continued practicing yoga after I began working as a journalist, and my interest in meditation persisted. Because I knew buddhism was all about meditation practice, I was eager to travel to the center in Scotland and ask the resident lama for instruction. It felt like an assignation that was long overdue.

The Victorian mansion that housed Samye Ling was cold and damp, and on my first morning I was ushered into the office of its director, an unsmiling Tibetan in a baggy suit called Akong Rinpoche. Akong seemed about as hospitable as the environment, and when I told him I wanted to learn to meditate he asked me in turn if I wanted to take refuge vows. I wasn't sure what this meant, but I knew it implied something about a formal commitment to buddhism. I told him this seemed premature and that I was really just curious about learning to meditate. He handed me a book, titled *Meditation in Action* by Chögyam Trungpa, and told me to read it. It seemed the interview was over, and I felt disappointed that I had traveled so far for such a meager response to my curiosity.

What should I read next? I asked.

There is another book, he said. It's called *Cutting Through Spiritual Materialism*. You can buy it in the bookstore.

And with that my introduction to Tibetan buddhism concluded.

I spent a week at Samye Ling and beyond reading the short book Akong had given me, I never did learn anything more about buddhism or meditation. There were no American girls in residence; in fact, there were virtually no guests at all except a young German guy and myself. Because yoga was my spiritual practice, I spent a chunk of time each morning practicing my *asanas*. Then I would take long walks across the rugged sheep pasture of the surrounding hills. The scenery was bleak and so was my mood. My curiosity about buddhism seemed misplaced, because it was clearly a foreign and inaccessible practice. In the main house, a Tibetan monk conducted a ceremony twice a day in a small, darkened shrine room. A handful of Western students seemed to know the liturgy and were able to follow along, but I didn't have a clue. At one point toward the end of the practice, which lasted about an hour, the monk led the recitation of a phrase which sounded like "Oh, monny bemoan" over and over. Only years later did I realize we were performing the *Chenrezig puja,* an offering to the bodhisattva of compassion whose mantra "Om Mani Pema Hung" is the national mantra of Tibet.

I did buy the second book recommended by Akong, and on the dust jacket noted that its author, Chögyam Trungpa, who had originally lived at Samye Ling, now lived in Boulder, Colorado. It explained that he had founded a college for artists, poets and buddhists called Naropa Institute, which sounded very cool. I also noted that when people at Samye Ling talked about Trungpa, they did so in hushed tones of veneration. I glanced at the book's contents, which were intimidating and clearly designed for people much further along in the study of buddhism than I. I had no plans to visit the United States and the notion of ever attending Naropa Institute seemed like a dream. I got on my motorcycle and set off back to the London suburbs and my job as a provincial journalist. I felt dispirited and lonely. En route, I ran over a nail at sixty miles per hour and blew out the rear tire. The back end of the bike yawed from side to side as I throttled back and tried to stay upright. I eventually came to a stop, my heart pounding. I laboriously fixed the flat, and when I set off again it was dark and very cold. All the rest of the way, I imagined the back end giving way again, without traction or support, which is precisely how my life felt in the winter of 1975.

five

The long motorcycle trip to Scotland did help resolve my plans for the future. I decided that when my commitment to the paper expired in July, I would quit my job and sell my motorcycle to finance a trip to the States. I had planned to visit for so long, after all, and it was clear that Tessa was not coming back any time soon. She was both encouraging and guarded. Her living arrangement had become complicated because she was now having an affair with Todd while working for him and his wife. I could plan to stay there but she was unsure how things would work out. I lied and claimed I had no particular expectations—I was just eager to break free from my provincial life and New Mexico sounded like the perfect destination for me, with or without Tessa as my partner. A month or so before I left, a distraught letter arrived containing an ominous warning. The situation with Todd and Celeste had become unworkable, and Todd had chosen his rich wife over his English lover. Tessa was devastated and had to find somewhere else to live. I still love you, she wrote, but in a different way. I can't wait to see you again. I held on to the second declaration while deliberately ignoring the first.

It was a thrill to finally arrive in the United States after so much antici-pation. After landing at JFK airport, I craned my neck at the featureless Queens neighborhoods on the drive into Manhattan—look at the size of the people! Look at their weird wooden houses! Through Richard's con-tacts I was planning to stay with a journalist in New Jersey, who met me at the celebrated information booth at Grand Central. Jet-lagged and over-stimulated, I felt like an extra in my own low-budget movie. Later that night, after further disorientation fueled by some ferocious Thai grass, I found myself tucked into a pullout bed with a glass of ginger ale and the Sonny and Cher show on TV. My grip on reality was fairly tenuous, however. Sonny and Cher would appear in cute skits, then the show would cut to commercials in which Sonny and Cher also appeared, selling Buicks and breakfast cereal. American culture felt impossibly alien to me.

By the time I made the cross-country trip to New Mexico I had become acclimated and genuinely exhilarated by the scale of these differences. To an Englishman, the continental U.S. is impossibly vast, and the very notion of driving for four days through different climatic and time zones is outrageous. I'd arranged a ride with a gay New Yorker named Frank who was relocating to San Francisco with his two cats. We shared driving, motel rooms and nonstop accounts of our different experiences. He was an addict of the zany TV show *Mary Hartman, Mary Hartman*, and we had to make a nightly tour of motels until we found one that carried the right station. He would roll around in helpless laughter at scenes that left me baffled and po-faced. During the day I would use my little camera to shoot totemic images from our trip: a massive, flat Cadillac looming in my side-view mirror; our car tethered to its self-pumping gas hose; the cartoon architecture of burgerdom. I particularly loved driving through the forests of Tennessee and found myself jotting ideas for poems, which I hadn't written in years. I guess I was experiencing my own soul expansion. As New Mexico grew closer, I began to confide in Frank my fears for my reunion with Tessa. He told me I was welcome to come along to San Francisco if things didn't work out. It was sweet of him but I knew as he dropped me in Santa Fe to hitchhike the last 50 miles that I would likely never see him again.

I wandered down the dusty dirt road to Todd's ranch in Embudo, New Mexico, late one afternoon in late July. A group of hippies with several young kids was sitting at a table in the shade outside an adobe ranch house, so I dropped my bag and joined them. They had been expecting me. Celeste, a wispy, freckled woman who was holding a toddler in her lap, offered me her hand. Todd, a tall hippie with a big blond moustache and ponytail, came over and kissed me on the crown of the head. Someone showed me where I could shower and take a nap. Tessa was living in the next valley in a cabin with no phone or electricity so we'd go find her after dinner, I was told. As I was drifting off into a welcome sleep, I heard what I thought was a rifle shot.

The first of many personal changes that summer occurred when I sat down later at the same shady table for dinner. There were about ten of us sharing a large cut of roasted meat—goat I was told. The meat tasted unpleasantly strong and fresh, and Todd explained that he had butchered the animal only a couple of hours earlier; this was the source of the rifle shot I'd heard earlier. I became vegetarian on the spot. Later we drove a few miles and found a darkened cabin down a long dirt road, but no one was home. I left a note for Tessa and returned to the ranch.

The next morning, I was hanging out my wash when I saw her walking down the driveway from the main road. I had not seen her in a year and a half, and she had changed. Her hair was long and loose and bleached by the sun. Her skin was the color of pecan. She wore a print halter, torn jeans and sandals and carried a can of Bugler tobacco. Always near-sighted, she approached me squinting to make sure who I was. We shared a long hug, a gesture my body recognized. She gave me a dry kiss on the mouth, a gesture I did not recognize.. Quickly, we repaired to the small clapboard guesthouse where I was staying where she made herb tea and rolled cigarettes. Her mood was somber.

Slowly, over the next day or so, the reasons became clear. Despite their decision to end their affair, Tessa was still in love with Todd—I think he represented all the physical and emotional liberation she'd experienced—and he still had feelings for her. Returning to his ranch was therefore very painful for her, but her plan was to stay there with me for the duration of my visit. She had moved in with Jack in the next valley, a guy she considered a good friend. There were other guests expected during the next two weeks in addition to me—her friend Julie from Boulder and, improbably, her mother and younger sister—and she dreaded having to put up a front for them. Apparently I did not present the same challenge.

I was stunned by the changes in her. She now spoke a patois of Home Counties English and hippiespeak, and sometimes I had to get her to clarify notions that she took for granted. (Karma, I remember, was one). Apparently, much of her predicament could be explained by the fact she was a Scorpio. But in addition to a broken heart, she was also suffering deep remorse. For the first time in her life, Tessa had been wild and bad and she was appalled at herself. She was able to tell me this because I knew her better than anyone and could provide some perspective for her. Quite how I did this escapes me now, because I was suffering my own acute sense of loss. It was clear from the first dry touch of her lips that our physical relationship was over, that we were no longer a couple. Her feelings had changed, and she loved another guy. She had clearly warned me, but I had come anyway. This was very tough for me. We shared a bed, and most of our waking time. We would forget our predicament occasionally and share moments of spontaneous connection, then inevitably I would be reminded of our separation. We weathered the visits of her guests together, but increasingly Tessa would sneak off to be alone with Todd. She had no emotional reserves for me, so I felt quite alone. She knew what she was putting me through but explained that she had not wanted to keep me away because that would deny me the experience of the place. Many of our Cambridge friends had made the long trek to New Mexico by now, and Tessa complimented me that, unlike others, I seemed able to hold my own in crucial areas like chainsaw use, drug consumption and metaphysical debate. Curiously, I was, and remain, extremely grateful for Tessa's decision to encourage my visit.

The paradoxical truth was that I was having a fabulous time. I had never experienced anything like the full-bore, back-to-the-land lifestyle of the American hippie during the heyday of the counterculture and it was truly exhilarating. There could never have been a parallel phenomenon in Britain—there was simply not enough land or enough money around to buy and cultivate it. But that's not the main reason. Generally speaking the educated classes in Britain are averse to working with their hands—it's part of the social hammerlock of the class system. Manual tasks are the province of the folks my sister affectionately calls the "oiks" (the primacy of voice accent again), the bum-crack cowboys who have been ripping off effete intellectuals like me since Chaucer's day. In New Mexico I met guys with advanced degrees who could butcher an animal, weld a pickup frame and build a house as well as riff on the meaning of life. In fact, this was the *norm*. The communal ethic meant that everyone pitched in together and I was quickly engaged in all kinds of construction projects for the first time. And the land was wild and beautiful; mountainous, semi-desert scrub with patches of intense cultivation in the valleys where the irrigation channels ran.

Our day at Todd and Celeste's ranch would start with the residents and hangers-on (there were probably a dozen of us) wandering down to the river in the nude to bathe. Luckily I am not uptight about this sort of thing and quickly got into the swing, so to speak, despite a milky skin that burns easily. The real naturalist, however, was Antler, who would sometimes inhale a joint, then swim across the twenty-foot wide Rio Grande and disappear to commune with the desert fauna on his own aboriginal walkabout. He was a big, hairy guy and would return hours later, scorched and beatific, looking like a walking bush with a cock in the middle.

During the day there were all kinds of communal projects: guys building additions or freestanding cabins out of adobe bricks with mud-and-straw cement. Precision didn't seem to be a big deal and everyone worked stoned. In the evenings there were bonfires, people to visit, even political meetings. At one bonfire party, the Banditos showed up. These were former Hells' Angels from California who had moved out to New Mexico and traded their Harleys for horses and rode around causing trouble. One skinny guy with a moustache and no front teeth strode into the firelight, pulled out a six-shooter and fired it in the air, demanding beer. He got some pretty quickly. I shook my head in awe.

Multiplicity of religious trips was part of the *gestalt*. One day a group of Jesus freaks showed up, with long hair, white robes and sandals, and accepted Todd's offer of a free meal (minus the goat meat.) I tried to engage one guy in conversation, but his gaze remained fixed on the horizon as he chewed slowly. I asked him about his philosophy, and he studied me for a moment. "No meat. No sex. No materialism," was his laconic reply. In Dixon, in the next valley, a group of hippie Muslims was observing Ramadan. The Yaqui Way of Knowledge presented in Carlos Castaneda's books was also popular. At one gathering, folks started discussing a spiritual center in nearby Taos called Lama Foundation. One woman recalled the visit several years earlier by Trungpa, the

Tibetan lama with the outrageous reputation. I thought about mentioning his center in Scotland that I'd visited the previous year, but let it go.

One night in my first week I attended a political rally hosted by
Chicano activists who belonged to *La Raza Unida*, a grassroots campaign that was trying to unseat the corrupt local sheriff. (I didn't think
sheriffs existed outside Hollywood.) The sheriff, whose name I remember was Emilio Naranjo, had retaliated against this effort by spraying
one guy's living room with automatic weapon fire, and planting a bale
of marijuana in another guy's trunk. To someone who only recently had
been covering the bring-and-buy sale of the local women's club, the description of such events elicited deep pleasure.

And I was writing a lot. Not just broken-hearted laments but more
ambitious stuff inspired by my new environment. I wrote poetry, a
prose journal, even a short play. Some I shared with Tessa and some
with Todd, who was a writer himself and had contributed to the hippie
Bible *The Whole Earth Catalog*. Todd sidestepped this fairly explicit invitation to discuss what we were both going through, and I felt that for
all his machismo, he was basically faint-hearted. I didn't like him or the
way he had treated Tessa, the way he was still trying to have his cake
and eat it. But, hey, I was probably biased.

Sadly, it was clear I could not stay in New Mexico indefinitely.
Tessa's moving back had stirred up things among Tessa, Todd and his
wife and I was increasingly in the way. I did not have the independent
connections in the community that might have allowed me to stay elsewhere. Despite the fact that I was having a blast, we both knew I had to
leave and eventually fixed on a date in mid-August. I decided to hitchhike north to Boulder to visit Julie, Tessa's friend who had stayed with
us for a week. It was my only other address in the entire country.

The day we drove north to Taos for me to start my trip I was filled
with a manic, gallows humor as a way to fend off my despair. This was
finally the end for Tessa and me, and I could not be sure I would ever see
her again. There was of course poetic justice in this outcome; I had sufficient grasp of karma to understand that. Now that she was unattain-
able, I would have committed to her wholeheartedly. But I had
prevaricated for so long that I had missed my chance. I had also physically left her many times, and although I was the one heading out, she

was now leaving me, and the circle was closed. We hugged, and then she was gone. I stuck out my thumb and almost immediately an archetypal VW bus filled with hippies pulled over. I climbed onto the mattresses in back and saw "Today is the first day of the rest of your life" scrawled on the wall of the van. It seemed particularly apt. Looking back on that trip to Boulder now, it seems that two realities were about to collide for me, and at the point of their impact, weird phenomena spilled out. I still can't accept that what followed was completely random.

The hippies told me they would take me to the New Mexico/Colorado state line where they lived on a commune, a journey of several hours. The predictable joints were passed around, and conversation fell silent. I became lulled by the note of the engine, and was aware that we were descending a long mountain pass. I may have even drifted into sleep.

Here we are, man, the driver shouted back to me as he pulled onto a dirt road.

I thanked them and climbed out, realizing I was still pretty stoned. I also realized as the van pulled away that I had I had been precisely wrong; that we had been *climbing* a long mountain pass, that I was now high up in the Rockies on a deserted highway. It was cold and the wind was howling; I started shivering and fished my jean jacket out of my pack. It was several minutes before any vehicle appeared, but mercifully the first one pulled over—a dirty white, low sedan that sprayed gravel as it braked. The driver shooed a dog onto the back seat and I climbed in quickly, hefting my pack onto my knee.

Thanks, I said, looking across at her.

Why? she responded, rolling her eyes and jamming her foot to the floor. The acceleration threw me back in my seat. Oh boy, what have we got into here? I wondered.

The driver was a middle-aged woman with wild hair, sloppy clothes and an erratic driving style. She also smelled of booze. The highway was empty and the car swung back and forth across the lanes. She was driving very fast.

I tried to make conversation but she ignored my pleasantries and told me she was not scared of me, because if she snapped her fingers, her dog would go for my throat. She held up her fingers in front of me to demonstrate. She had a strong German accent. I glanced in the back seat and saw the dog was a German shepherd that was watching me closely.

Where you go? she asked.

Walsenburg, I replied quickly, knowing it was the next town.

I go to Denver. You not go to Denver?

No, I lied.

I am friends with the Walsenburg chief of police, she said. He give me permit for this, she said, reaching under the cushion on which she was sitting and retracting a large pistol, which she waved in the air.

Will you put that away? I asked, really scared now.

She put the pistol back under her cushion and looked across at me, her tone changing.

Where you from?

England.

You a nice boy. You want to come to Denver and stay with me?

I have to get out in Walsenburg, I repeated.

Now my heart was really pounding and I turned my attention to the road. She was still driving really fast and seemed to be unable to keep the car in one lane. We kept veering across toward the median, then she would over-correct and we would head back toward the shoulder. I wondered about reaching over to steady the wheel but thought that if I did so the dog might attack me. I realized I might not get out of this car alive.

Maybe I should drive, I suggested.

We there soon, she replied.

We passed the sign for the Walsenburg city limits and approached an overpass. The car swung again toward the median and she didn't appear to be correcting the wheel as we headed for central bridge support. When we were ten yards away I panicked, reached over and yanked on the wheel to avoid a collision.

Pull over. Pull over. I'll drive, I yelled.

Miraculously, a diner and gas station appeared on our right just past the bridge.

Pull in there, I ordered.

She slowed, turned off and pulled up at the gas pumps. As soon as the car came to a halt I opened the door and stumbled out with my pack. I looked back at her.

I'm getting out here, lady. You're a psycho, I said, ducking and running toward the diner, half expecting her to fire off a round at me.

A peppy teenage girl at the counter asked me what I'd like.

I asked for water and asked her whether the white car was still waiting at the pumps.

Yeah, she said. What's wrong?

I told her the driver had tried to kill me, but she thought I was kidding.

Is it still there? I asked.

Yes.

Tell me when it leaves.

The white car idled for about ten minutes until it drove off. I stayed at the counter for an hour or so to be sure she was gone. The place was mostly empty and the waitress's bright chatter calmed me. Gradually my nerves steadied and I realized I had to continue my journey. By now it was late afternoon as I set off to walk the mile into downtown Walsenburg. Denver was four hours away and I thought I could make it that night if I was lucky.

The sun was still high and warm on my face. As I approached the center of town I saw the cars were slowing to avoid a brown shape in the middle of the road, which from a distance looked like a large grocery sack. As I got closer, I saw it was in fact the carcass of a German shepherd. I saw no blood, but it was obviously dead. I immediately thought of the dog on the back seat of the white car and quickened my step. A hundred yards further on, a man stumbled out of a doorway and spoke to me angrily. He was not drunk but seemed mentally retarded, because he could not pronounce words distinctly. He held a very large steel bolt in his hand that he shook at me threateningly. Now I broke into a run.

At the edge of town I decided to get a motel room—the prospect of hitchhiking further that day was impossible. I sat shaking on the bed, wondering what the hell I had done to generate the spate of evil omens I had just encountered. I was at an extremely low point, and reflected that if today was the first day of the rest of my life, things were not looking so good. The next day I hitchhiked on to Denver without incident, took the bus to Boulder and called Julie. She and her husband lived in Nederland, a mountain town at the top of Boulder canyon, a wild and funky place compared with chic, middle-class Boulder. She drove me up the mountain pass through an angry storm that abated as we drove into town.

After showering and changing I told Julie the scary stories of my trip. Her husband Tom was tending the grill on the deck.

Hey, look at this ! he called out to us.

An intense rainbow, the most vivid I had ever seen, had sprung up from the Barker reservoir dam at the head of the canyon and was extending down the valley toward Boulder.

Julie knew that Tessa and I had split up and squeezed my arm.

Maybe it means your karma is changing, she said.

six

The Forks general store on Route 287 north of Fort Collins is the first
contact you make with the outer world after you leave Rocky Mountain
Dharma Center (now renamed Shambhala Mountain Center). I've
stopped there many times, and on that August afternoon in 1976 after
my first encounter with Trungpa Rinpoche, I stopped to call Tessa in
New Mexico. She was working in the garden and came to the phone after a brief delay. She sounded really pleased to hear from me.

Hey, how're you doing? Julie said you'd gone off to meditate. How
was that?

Enlightening. It was really amazing, Tess.

Wow. What are you going to do now?

I'm going to try and get work in Canada, save some money and
come back here. What about you?

Brenda and I are going to take off for Central America. It's kinda
weird here. I can't figure out where I'd live this winter.

How long for?

We probably have enough money for a month or two.

Then back to England?

I suppose so.

Well, stay in touch.

Of course. Hey Tone, you sound great.

I feel great.

Bye now.

Bye.

I have a favorite snapshot taken in London right after I came back from
that trip in 1976 (the Canada plan quickly fell through). I am standing

with my elder sister in her backyard; we are both very young, in our twenties (although she already has two kids and a mortgage). I have long hair, a moustache and am wearing coveralls (known as dungarees in England) and a necklace. I also have a big grin, because although I am broke and homeless, I have some direction in my life for the first time. I'm going to become a buddhist. Of course, becoming buddhist does not mean you've resolved anything about work or relationships; my elation springs more from the conviction that I've discovered something meaningful to which I can make a commitment. It came as a big relief.

Cambridge friends from the *Broadsheet* era soon helped me work out the living and working stuff. I took over John's job teaching English at a tutorial college and moved into Gordon's squat in South London. The squatters' movement in London in the 1970s deserves a word or two, because it was probably the closest thing we Brits had to a back-to-the-land movement, although exclusively an urban phenomenon. Bizarre English property laws together with medieval statutes governing adverse possession (we were fond of quoting the Forcible Entry Act of 1381) meant that enterprising folks like us (and thousands of others) could occupy vacant housing and not be evicted without a court order. In the Sixties and Seventies, the municipal authorities in London were committed to redeveloping huge swaths of Victorian row houses that they considered substandard. However, the property would often remain vacant for years while the necessary plans, permits and funding were secured. If you could break into a vacant house without being seen, you could claim "squatters rights" if the cops showed up, so long as you had a mattress on the floor. And the houses weren't substandard as far as we were concerned. Anything with a sound roof and floors could be inhabited because we could cobble together the wiring and plumbing even if it had been ripped out by scavengers. It made it possible to live in London—then and now a very expensive place—on next to nothing. The council would usually wait for months or even years to begin eviction proceedings. In the 1970s a whole subculture flourished around this anarchic lifestyle.

Trying to practice buddhism in London in this era was frustrating, because there was not much happening yet. I went to the celebrated Buddhist Society in Pimlico for talks on Tibetan buddhism, but the gatherings seemed to me like a throwback to the spiritualist church of my teens—middle-aged eccentrics sitting around in the dark, then listening to arcane presentations on tantra. I did discover a meditation center in a former orphanage near Cambridge run by a lama who had originally come to England with Chögyam Trungpa. Lama Chime Rinpoche was a tall, angular Tibetan who was married to an English-woman and worked at the British Museum. At Kham House, periods of silent meditation alternated with pujas conducted in Tibetan like at Samye Ling; however, here the liturgy was transliterated into English so at least you could participate. And unlike Akong Rinpoche, Lama Chime was warm and welcoming and granted interviews readily. I visited frequently, although I still yearned for the ruggedness and directness of Trungpa Rinpoche's approach and my commitment to return to Boulder was unwavering. That winter I wrote him a letter, knowing it was unlikely he would personally see it, mentioning our discussion and his offer to help me return. I told him I wanted to study at Naropa Institute and join his community.

One development that could have deflected my intent was Tessa's return. She came back in late October after traveling through Mexico, Guatemala and Belize, but kept a low profile for a while, staying with her parents and rarely venturing into the city. She was still bruised from her experience in New Mexico and was uncharacteristically subdued for a long time. We saw each other occasionally, but then she and Brenda found substitute teaching jobs in North London and moved in with my sister, of all people. My feelings for her had not really moved on, and we naturally began to spend more time together. She had developed her own interest in buddhism and came with me when I took my refuge vows with Lama Chime at Kham House. Neither of us was interested in other people and the prospect of renewing our relationship inevitably arose. One weekend she agreed to stay with me in South London but then at the last minute changed her mind. Crestfallen, I went home alone. Later that week she wrote me a letter that said, "I can't be your lover again. I don't know why. I shudder at some of the things I've put you through." It was a first acknowledgement of the pain of the New Mexico experience for both of us, but typically, it was declared in a letter, not face-to-face. However, it was a declaration I have always respected, because an easier path would have been to fake a response and resume our relationship. She knew, as I think I secretly did, that any such course was doomed; the growth we both still needed would not occur inside our relationship.

It was a cold, lonely winter and my spirits inevitably ebbed. In February I was buoyed by the response I got from Naropa Institute, offering me a work-study position for the following summer so I could take classes for free. In the Spring I visited a new buddhist center in the north of England called Manjushri Institute that had been founded by two charismatic lamas whose teaching I had read and admired. However, the traditional style there did not suit me at all, and I came out of talks feeling more depressed than inspired. Tessa sounded very interested in the place and I told her to check it out—it was definitely authentic if unsuited to my personal style.

By the time June rolled around and my teaching commitment expired, I was overripe to return to Colorado. I liquidated everything I could and even borrowed a little money from my father, convinced that if things worked out, I would not be returning. My commitment to buddhism, which I had feared might be a flash in the pan, had survived and even flourished, and as my plane back to the States accelerated down the runway, my whole being felt a surge of excitement.

The person who deserves the most credit for my return to the United States is not Chögyam Trungpa, but Wendy Layton. I will have more to say about Wendy, but in brief, this person is a star, well known and widely adored throughout the far-flung Shambhala International community, which is what Trungpa Rinpoche's successor organization is now called. She is my oldest and truest friend in the dharma, without whose support I could not have made my way in the United States at all. At the first meal break at Rocky Mountain Dharma Center in 1976, I had spotted her seated on the grass outside the kitchen building, eating alone. She was small and cute and friendly and we soon struck up a rapport. She had also come to the program without arranging anywhere to stay, so I offered—generously, I felt, on my part—to let her sleep in my tent. My level of sexual frustration after the New Mexico experience was pretty high, but I couldn't figure how to contrive any realistic contact through our thick sleeping bags in a chilly tent, or even whether such advances were in order. But Wendy, recently arrived in Boulder herself, was gracious and full of information about Trungpa Rinpoche and his community, and our connection grew steadily stronger. She had to leave early to go back to work and offered to let me stay with her in Boulder after the end of the program.

I accepted this invitation and the night we spent together strengthened our connection and fortified my decision to return. We stayed in touch throughout the following year, exchanging letters and gifts, and she generously offered to let me stay at her apartment when I came back to Boulder as a Naropa student. A lot has been written about the ferment surrounding the start of Naropa Institute in 1974, when Trungpa Rinpoche and his students planned for a gathering of five hundred and two thousand showed up. Rinpoche and the Western guru Ram Dass taught on alternate nights, and a host of big names from the worlds of poetry, dance, psychology and philosophy came to teach classes and join the dialogue. The energy was similar in 1977, although Trungpa Rinpoche himself was not there—he was in retreat in Massachusetts. Spiritual leadership of the summer institute had been conferred on Maezumi Roshi, a Japanese Zen master from Los Angeles, and a fellow called Ösel Tendzin, an Italian-American from New Jersey who had been appointed Trungpa Rinpoche's "regent" or successor the previous year. I knew nothing of this guy's existence before returning to Boulder, but I liked him from the start. He was buoyant and expansive and had a forthright teaching style I really appreciated. He dressed weirdly, though. He wore expensive suits and shiny shoes like a banker, which was incongruous in the shaggy, tie-dyed atmosphere of Naropa's summer program. What I soon learned was that the buddhist community, at Rinpoche's insistence, had shed its hippie accoutrements and entered its "corporate phase." People now dressed conservatively, and Rinpoche's organization was run along the business model with a board of directors, department heads and the like. The leadership was exclusively male. This top-down bureaucracy was established in response to the explosive growth of Rinpoche's community in the early Seventies, but was also likely favored because it most closely replicated the hierarchical administration of Tibetan monasteries in which Rinpoche himself had been trained. The conservative style of dress reflected his personal preference for formality and precision in comportment and manners. Both these aspects of the Boulder community were tough for me to adjust to at first.

My style of involvement with Ösel Tendzin in the beginning was the same as with Trungpa Rinpoche. I asked questions at the end of his talks to clarify points but also to get noticed. Within a few weeks I was pretty sure he knew who I was, and we developed a good-natured connection. Later I would get to know him quite well.

I gravitated naturally toward the poets, a high-profile group at Naropa thanks to Allen Ginsberg, founder of the institute's Jack Kerouac School of Disembodied Poetics. Ginsberg, a former Hindu, had become an early student of Trungpa Rinpoche after a chance meeting when they both hailed the same taxi in New York City in 1972. They had an extremely close bond and collaborated extensively throughout their lives. Ginsberg's prominence meant that the Naropa writing faculty was filled with marquee names like Burroughs, Corso and Kesey from the Beat generation, but also those of the more intellectual poets I liked such as Dorn and Creeley. I took classes with both Ed Dorn and Allen Ginsberg that first summer, and it was a blast to have my work critiqued by such titans. Ginsberg's class was particularly delightful. It consisted mainly of Allen's reminiscence about events that had generated literature that I held dear to my heart, like Kerouac's *Dharma Bums* and *The Subterraneans*. He would ramble at length about his tortured love for Neal Cassady and the events that became *On the Road*. Allen had very little sense of self-importance, and his class was informal and conversational. He was also very authoritative on writers he considered forebears like Blake and Whitman, quoting long passages from memory to illustrate how both the vision and style of the Beats had been foreshadowed in the Western canon.

The central event of the week for the poets was the Wednesday night poetry reading in the main auditorium. Hundreds of people showed up and the atmosphere was festive and subversive—no business suits on display on these occasions. After one of the early readings, a guy from class told me about a party that night at the home of the couple who taught Tai Chi at the institute. After quaffing a couple of beers at a local bar with friends, I decided to check it out. The first thing you noticed when you got to the party was that it was very crowded and predominantly male. The second thing you noticed was that most people were naked. The house had a hot tub on the back porch and folks were undressing, soaking, then neglecting to get dressed afterward. I wandered out back and saw that Allen was holding court in the tub along with his long-time partner, Peter Orlovsky. As I've said, I'm not particularly uptight about this sort of thing so I shed my clothes and climbed in.

Allen typically had a coterie of young male admirers from whom he chose his boyfriends, and there were two or three in the tub with Allen and Peter. Allen recognized me immediately from class and advanced toward me across the tub, his wide nostrils flaring above the water surface like a hippo's. Where is he going to put his hands? I wondered. They came to rest on my knees. He asked about my background, and we began to chat. I started to get a little uncomfortable but was saved by a strange, ungainly woman from class who was something of a Beat poet groupie. She arrived on the back porch, and squawking with delight, threw off her clothes and hurled herself into the tub with a belly flop. All the men quickly got out. Allen and I resumed our conversation on the shag rug indoors. We were still nude but I felt less vulnerable out in the open. I was able to ask him what Kerouac was *really* like. He said Kerouac had been much misunderstood in his later, conservative years, and was always a very gentle soul. This tribute became all the more extraordinary to me when I later read how Kerouac, in his final alcoholic years, would regularly phone Ginsberg and excoriate him with anti-Semitic slurs, then refuse to answer his door when Allen tried to visit him at his mother's house on Long Island. Allen's loyalty toward his friends and his tireless advocacy of their work throughout their lives were truly remarkable.

The summer institute numbered some members from the Boulder sangha among its students and staff, but many of my new contacts were transplants from the coasts, particularly from New York City. The creative energy was ceaseless; there were lectures, performances and readings every night of the week, and I was quickly involved with writing and producing student publications. I was also taking classes in buddhism from some of Trungpa Rinpoche's senior American students. I felt excited to be involved in something as dynamic and eclectic as Naropa Institute, and proud that Trungpa Rinpoche and his students had created it. I was particularly impressed that you did not need to be a buddhist to feel welcome or to take part. In fact, most of the poets were skeptical about buddhism and openly hostile toward Trungpa Rinpoche himself. Not all the poets liked each other either; Allen Ginsberg told me that Dorn had agreed to teach, "even though he thinks I'm a faggot and a cocksucker."

As the summer wound down I made the decision to stay and take my chances in Boulder. The prospect was daunting on one level because I had no legal status and many of the friends I'd made that summer were about to head back East. But the sense of belonging to something big and important outweighed everything else, and there was nothing comparable waiting for me in England, a culture that by contrast seemed timid and constricted. A Canadian friend who was leaving for Karmê-Chöling, the meditation center in Vermont, told me I could take over his job as a bookkeeper for a sangha business if I knew how to count to ten. Because I would be cutting the checks, I could pay myself under the table, as he had done. Through other friends I found a share in a trailer park for next to nothing. So I let my return ticket expire, bought a down jacket at the thrift store and got ready for my first Boulder winter.

seven

It was a slower pace of life in Boulder after the Naropa summer program ended in 1977, but the transition was made easier because the sangha was large and well organized with a clear program of activities for new members like me. Classes were held in the evenings in people's homes and there were regular, three-hour periods of sitting meditation at the main center downtown. Each new member was assigned an older student as a meditation instructor; there was even a "practice requirement" to maintain membership. I attended classes and group meditation faithfully because I was eager both to learn and to meet new people. My friendships within the community expanded rapidly that fall, and I was impressed by the people I was meeting. The Boulder sangha was for the most part close to my age, inquisitive and good-humored, and unified by a tremendous devotion to both Trungpa Rinpoche and the regent Ösel Tendzin. I soon moved from the trailer park to a shared apartment with other sangha members and quickly felt like I'd made a genuine home in Boulder. My job as a rookie bookkeeper paid a few hundred dollars a month, enough to feed and house me, and I never for a minute second-guessed my decision to stay.

The growth of my buddhist understanding and commitment paralleled my experience during the seminar with Rinpoche the previous summer. There was significant instruction in the doctrinal aspects of the dharma (the Sanskrit term meaning "the law," "the way things are," or often, simply, "the teachings of the Buddha.") This was absorbed not by studying the sutras—the Buddha's original teachings—themselves, but the commentaries that Rinpoche's early books and the transcripts of talks that he had given comprised. This was very welcome, for although I had regularly attended retreat centers during my year in England, there had been no consistent program of study for me to follow. As at RMDC, my sessions of study in Boulder were supported by a requirement to meditate a lot. These are the complementary components of the buddhist path—study and practice, intellect and intuition, or neuroscientifically speaking, the left brain and right brain perspectives.

I'm disinclined to expound the basic teachings of buddhism here—essentially, they concern the psychology of ego and its self-preservation instincts of passion, aggression and ignorance. The teachings on impermanence and emptiness are also important. These teachings struck me then, as now, as logical and pretty much irrefutable, requiring not so much belief as a call to action. This action suggested I be kinder to myself and more compassionate to others, which in turn required that I make a commitment to meditation practice. These discoveries were thrilling to me, the fruition of my connection to yoga that had begun my recovery after the experience in Belfast.

I was among the hundreds of students who went to Stapleton airport in Denver to welcome Rinpoche back from his one-year retreat in December 1977. Seeing him again gave me a great surge of joy, and Rinpoche himself looked radiant. He was dressed formally in a dark suit, overcoat and fur hat, looking something like an Eskimo businessman. On seeing him I was reminded of his disability, the partial paralysis on his left side that gave him a pronounced limp. It had been so long since I'd seen him that I had forgotten. We accompanied him to his car and then all drove back to Boulder for a welcoming ceremony. There were hundreds of us packed into the Boulder shrine room, and as a neophyte member of this large group I wondered how I would be able to cultivate anything like a personal connection to him.

By 1977, the pioneering days of Rinpoche's early life in the United States were long past—he had a big organization, thousands of students throughout North America and centers in most American cities. Of course, stories of those early years were basic sangha lore and I was quite familiar with them. In early 1970, Rinpoche and his young wife Diana had moved from Montreal to an old farmhouse in northern Vermont that American students from Samye Ling had bought for him. From this base, he began teaching first on the East Coast, then in Colorado and California, eventually settling in Boulder in 1972. The unruly energy of these early years has been well chronicled, notably in Diana Mukpo's and Jeremy Hayward's memoirs. The main change from the years in Scotland was that no longer was Trungpa Rinpoche a remote, mysterious figure in exotic garb. During these early years Rinpoche basically hung out with his students, dressing like them, learning to talk like them, drinking and taking drugs like them, and having affairs like them. In the United States, Trungpa Rinpoche got to start over teaching Westerners, and his approach this time was revolutionary. With the fearlessness that characterized the rest of his life, he abandoned both the protection and privacy of his clerical status and plunged into the lifestyle of his American students until he understood it completely, uncannily, exquisitely. Then patiently and with great skill he set about molding his community into how an enlightened Western society might manifest.

But by 1977, the hippie era in Boulder was long past. Starting with the first visit by the 16th Karmapa in 1974 (the senior lama who had recognized the young Trungpa tulku in infancy), the sangha had been encouraged to express its sense of appreciation for the buddhist teachings through prevailing social norms. This implied adopting greater formality in grooming, dress and speech, a transition that most folks were able to make with remarkable ease. After some initial skepticism, it came as a welcome change for me, because it felt *right* to wear a suit and tie to hear Rinpoche speak, and it felt *right* to address my sangha brothers and sisters as Mr. or Ms. So-and-So. (This, of course, was how Rinpoche himself dressed, and how he addressed us.) Somehow the formality expressed our sense of appreciation in a palpable way, the way that performing traditional chants and supplications in English also did. Altogether I felt more alert, receptive and adult than I had ever felt to date, and began to notice that my knee-jerk reaction toward conservatism in general began to abate. With Rinpoche back among us there was a sense of marvelous, unlimited potential and that Boulder truly was the center of something important.

I had one big obstacle, however, and that was with an outfit called the Dorje Kasung, or the Vajra Guards. The first time I had ever laid eyes on Rinpoche at the final talk at Naropa Institute in 1976, he was wearing a blue blazer and gray slacks, as were several of his attendants who took up positions near the stage and around the auditorium. I knew that this was not a mere fashion statement, and I found the uniforms creepy and the presence of so many bodyguards disturbing. When I returned to Boulder the following year, I learned that this aspect of his organization was called the Dorje Kasung (literally "indestructible protectors of the teachings" in Tibetan). The group had come into formal existence with the first visit of Karmapa in 1974. A team of volunteers was enlisted to oversee transportation, crowd control and the physical safety of Karmapa during his visit. After his departure, the group continued to offer these services to Trungpa Rinpoche himself. Such protection is not unusual among the Tibetan hierarchy. Senior lamas, including the Dalai Lama and Karmapa, travel with parties of attendants of whom one or more are responsible for the teacher's physical safety. As Trungpa Rinpoche's unconventional reputation and teaching activity expanded, so did the need to provide security. Also, because of his disability, he needed help with many basic physical tasks. But whereas the bodyguards of Tibetan lamas are indistinguishable from the general party of attendant monks, Trungpa Rinpoche, with characteristic daring and creativity, made his guards distinct and separate, eventually formulating an entire teaching around their activity. He designed their uniforms, formulated their code of conduct and developed a whole path of training with which I was eventually to have my own vivid encounter. But in my first year in Boulder I was fairly hung up on the guard thing and was unsure what to do about it.

Like most of the Sixties generation, I had a visceral distrust of militarism, which was magnified by America's shameful adventure in Vietnam. I had also witnessed firsthand the cavalier trampling of civilian rights by the British army in Belfast. Even closer to home, I had my own peculiar and conflicted experience with the quasi-military shenanigans of the Boy Scouts. For reasons I have difficulty explaining, I stayed in the Boy Scouts from age eleven until the age of eighteen, eventually becoming the British equivalent of an Eagle Scout. All the while I loathed its regimentation and was particularly miserable at formal "camps" in which squads competed in every area from personal grooming to soccer games. I found this requirement humiliating and odious, and saw the

Dorje Kasung as a similar perversion, with their uniforms, their special salutes and their corny "reminder" slogans. My aversion became quite an obstacle during my first year in Boulder, and after Rinpoche came back from retreat, I decided to do something about it. I joined.

I did not know any members of the kasung personally so it was quite a leap for me to go down to the basement office in the community building in Boulder. I think the duty officer (yes, there were such formal ranks) was quite impressed with my reasons for enlisting and signed me up right away. I, too, was and remain proud of my decision to join. In my own meager way, I felt I was emulating my teacher who had embraced the messy, neurotic stew of the Seventies counterculture with such fearlessness. By now I also trusted him completely and was curious to find out what the hell this bizarre buddhist military thing was all about. I may also have felt that my being a guard might bring more physical proximity to him, but this was definitely a secondary motivation.

Like everything I encountered in Trungpa Rinpoche's world, once I was an active member of the Dorje Kasung I found that their procedures were intelligent, thorough and inspiring. There was typically a detail of up to eight guards at any public event, and each member had a specific role. There was both extensive briefing and debriefing. I found I appreciated the dedication and camaraderie of the group—it was comprised of men and women who were content to serve anonymously and selflessly in order to facilitate Trungpa Rinpoche's teaching. The activity was selfless because the essence of guarding meant that you did not participate in the event. You remained aloof and attentive to the environment, maintaining eye contact with one another, observing the audience. This inevitably meant that you could pay little attention to what Rinpoche might be saying. At community events at our center, the environment presented little if any threat, and the kasung presence was largely symbolic. At public talks in the yawning auditorium during Rinpoche's 1978 Naropa lectures, it was a different story. Hundreds of people showed up and all manner of folks could and did waylay him on his way to and from the stage. Rinpoche would always stop to talk. I spent one whole lecture on the roof of the building, peering through a skylight at his figure far below, supposedly scanning the adjacent roofs and balconies for snipers. If such precautions seemed over the top, it was a fact that

Rinpoche received threats and on at least one occasion a guy got into the administration building with explosives in a backpack.

The most gratifying shifts I had during this same period were as house guard at Rinpoche's home, which by now was known as Kalapa Court. It was a huge pile on University Hill, where Rinpoche lived with his eldest son Ösel (his wife Diana was studying dressage in Europe). Also in residence were the Regent and his wife Lila and their two sons—and this was just upstairs. In the basement lived several household staff, including the improbable John Perks, who may have been briefly single when I first met him. Perks, who was Rinpoche's valet and ran his household service, was such an unlikely figure he was practically a fictional character. Like a butler from a Gilbert and Sullivan operetta, he was a gangly Edwardian with a handlebar moustache, protruding teeth and a prominent Adam's apple. Although he had lived in the States since his teens, he was as British as Prince Charles and his manners were about as affected. We took an immediate liking to each other, and he may in fact have been instrumental in encouraging me to join the kasung. He tagged me immediately as a "Bolshie," which was accurate enough, whereas he, naturally, was an ardent monarchist. He ran Rinpoche's household like it was an English manor during the heyday of the aristocracy, and was very influential in both the style and substance of Rinpoche's personal tastes. He had an infectious sense of fun, and we got along famously from the very start.

In his autobiography *Born in Tibet*, Rinpoche writes that as a young student, he loved his teacher so much that he would sleep in the corridor outside his room. The house guard's role was similar. After the members of the household finally turned in, the guard broke out some makeshift bedding and slept in the hallway by the front door. I was very happy to do this. It felt right and natural to sleep by the door of the house where these two men whom I had come to love so much lived. The pleasure was compounded by the morning apparition of Perks, always up early no matter what time the evening had ended. In shirtsleeves, regimental tie and a smart apron, he would rustle up kippers (where did he get *those?*), eggs and coffee and host the overnight guard to a morning feast. There in the kitchen, as the house slept on, he and I would share our clandestine English breakfast, both bemoaning and delighting in our exile.

eight

That winter I also sat my first cabin retreat since joining the community. As I've mentioned, as a student of Trungpa Rinpoche, you were expected to sit a lot, in both group situations and alone. So right after Christmas in 1977 I revisited Rocky Mountain Dharma Center to sit my first solitary retreat. In this era, RMDC was largely a summer facility, and the retreat master was the only person on the premises when I showed up through the snow drifts in my ancient Chevy. He helped me get my gear and supplies up to the tiny, dirt-floor cabin behind the rocky outcrop called Marpa Point. The altitude was about 8500 feet, the temperature about minus ten. As he was leaving, the retreat master said to me playfully, Watch out for the bears!

It took a while for me to calibrate the woodstove to a setting where I was not sitting unclothed, like a fakir in my underwear. When it got dark, I began to get uneasy (I have never enjoyed the onset of darkness in retreat). But I fixed myself some stew from the freezer (a milk crate buried in the snow outside the front door), did my evening chants and went to bed. That's when the animal noises started. Loud and distinctive, the scraping and clawing sounds seemed to emanate from directly behind my head. I thought I heard grunts and heavy breathing. With pounding heart I imagined a bear pawing through my makeshift freezer, wolfing down the supplies I had brought. But now, ravenous and aroused, the beast was trying to break into the cabin! The sounds continued, louder and louder. I was bathed in sweat. What would I do if the creature broke down the door? There was an ax by the stove! Yes, I would grab the ax and defend myself! No, maybe I should smash my way out of a window! Some hours later the sounds abated and I finally drifted into sleep, consoling myself with the knowledge that the fresh snow would allow me to identify whatever had been prowling around outside.

I awoke to a blinding light flooding the cold cabin. When I had lit the stove and dressed, I stumbled outside to learn the worst. Nothing! The freezer was intact, the snow unmarked. Sheepishly remembering that bears hibernate, I came back inside and inspected the cabin. I had left the remains of the stew in its pan, covered with tinfoil, on a shelf in the kitchen area. Mice had systematically gnawed through the foil and devoured the contents, a noisy business indeed, although of a different order of threat than in my imagination. Thus abashed, I joined the fraternity of fearless yogis, alone in my mountain fastness.

Meditating for a week alone in a cabin is extremely boring. I had obeyed the admonition to bring only one book—a dharma book—with me, so there was nothing to do except meditate. Given the conditions, even exploring outdoors was out of the question. Between fifty-minute periods of sitting (the length of time it took an incense stick to burn down) I would walk around the inside of the A-frame cabin; two steps in one direction, three in the other, two more again, and so on, for ten hours a day. The only entertainment I had was my mind, which despite my commitment to the technique I'd learned (acknowledging thoughts, allowing them to dissolve, following the outbreath), responded to my physical confinement with tidal waves of fantasy. My brother-in-law, who became a practicing buddhist about ten years after me and quickly became a full-fledged yogi, sent me a cartoon composed during his first extended sitting experience. It consisted of a transection of his head, with a movie projector and screen in front labeled "Porno," a locked chest in back labeled "Regrets" and a tiny teardrop near the brain stem labeled "buddhanature." That just about captures it, although in my case there was also a long-running movie entitled "Heroic Boyhood Adventures Starring Me." Some days it felt absolutely hopeless—my mind a wild animal, untamable. Other days there was some kind of exhaustion, and a measure of respite from intense mental activity. Overall, the experience was challenging, and I felt a big sense of relief when the week was up and it was time to head back to Boulder.

The retreat master had told me he'd pick me up by one, but as the sun started to get low in the sky I realized he wasn't coming. The walk back to the main building was probably a mile or so through fairly deep snow, so I set out to beat the encroaching darkness. When I arrived, the staff greeted me like Shackleton appearing on Elephant Island long after he'd been given up for dead.

Where did you come from? Hey, you're Tony Cape, aren't you?

Yeah. I've been in retreat. Didn't Dennis tell you?

We didn't know anyone was here. He went down to Boulder yesterday. What do you want?

The retreat's over. Can someone get my gear?

We'll try and start the truck. It was forty below last night, with the wind chill.

Tell me about it.

I drank tea while the staff figured out how to retrieve my gear. I was amazed at how speedy and irritable they all seemed. I had slowed to an underwater pace, a development I had not noticed until I interacted with people who were still tuned to a normal wavelength. This struck me as both unexpected and hilarious. I drove back to Boulder at about thirty miles an hour. As I've noticed since, the effects of extended practice last for several days, before wearing off.

I did not develop strong personal relationships with either Rinpoche or the Regent during this era, although I saw a lot of both. They were probably away from Boulder about half the time, but when they were in town they were quite accessible. There were formal teachings at the Boulder center, at RMDC, and at Naropa Institute, but in addition there was a host of social events—vow ceremonies, community meetings, wedding receptions, birthday parties—that they regularly attended. It was a very social scene, and there was an intimate sense that they both belonged to us and with us. Of course, there was much jockeying for access, but I did not feel it necessary to push myself forward in any particular way. I would often connect with them naturally at this event or the other.

My friendship with John Perks led to some unusual encounters. One of his crackpot schemes was to introduce cricket as a way to civilize the colonials (again, how and where did Perks score a kitbag of cricket equipment?) Typically, he got Rinpoche to sign off on the endeavor, and had us all invited to a gala reception at Kalapa Court to inaugurate his scheme. There were enough British expatriates in the sangha to at least give it a shot, and we all showed up in our cricket whites to share toasts with Rinpoche in his living room ("Jolly good show!" was one of his favorite exhortations.) I sat next to him during this event and again found myself spontaneously connecting with him physically, this time holding his hand while we chatted, about what I can no longer remember. I didn't feel it necessary to say, "You know, I'm that English guy you made fun of two summers ago." I just figured he knew. At the end of the cricket season, Perks organized an outdoor Indian feast with Rinpoche, at which we ate off banana leaves with our fingers.

One aspect of the Boulder community that I was really grateful for in this era was that you did not need much money to be able to fully participate. For the first three years I subsisted on really quite little, in part because rents were cheap, as was admission to community events. I could usually volunteer for the kitchen crew at bigger programs at RMDC, which got me in for free, and there was always a way to be included in whatever was going on. Because I worked for a business owned by sangha members, there was never an issue with taking time off. A generation later, all this has changed. It's now very hard to work part-time and devote the rest of your life to studying dharma, as I did. I understand the reasons why this is so, but it's too bad. I often wonder whether the whole counterculture was not facilitated by the low cost of living that preceded the crushing inflation of the early 80s.

Despite his disability, Rinpoche taught tirelessly during his life in America, and I heard him lecture countless times during my first three-year stay in Boulder. The format was always the same. We would assemble at the prescribed time (typically eight p.m. for an evening talk), then we would sit and wait, usually for up to two hours. There was an implicit understanding that we "earned" the right to hear him teach by practicing meditation, the discipline he had taught us, for an extended time. The conditions were never ideal because the room was usually packed and latecomers would come and go as the time for the actual talk approached. (Annoyingly, members of the hierarchy would reserve the front rows of cushions in front of his chair and would show up just moments before Rinpoche himself.) The cue for his arrival was the appearance of the kusung, carrying the tray with the decanter of sake, glass and gold fan—constant fixtures on Rinpoche's teaching table. People would begin to fidget in anticipation, then the chant leader would ring the gong for us to stand as Rinpoche entered the hall.

Leaning on the forearm of his kasung, Rinpoche, always dressed in a business suit in this era, would walk slowly to the shrine platform, climb the four steps and advance to meet the shrine master in front of the enormous, deep orange shrine table. Together they would light candles and incense and offer them to the giant *thangka* or traditional painting of the Buddha above the shrine. Then Rinpoche would retreat slowly to his magnificent, lacquered teaching chair, eventually sitting heavily and gazing out at us. Then in turn, we would all sit. There might be announcements and introductory chants (in English). Rinpoche would slowly drink from his sake glass during this process, reach for his fan, clear his throat and begin speaking.

Reports of his physical being before his car accident concur that he had a light, ethereal presence. Trungpa Rinpoche during his teaching career in North America was as immoveable as a mountain. He was short and broad with a wide face that broke repeatedly into the broad grin of someone wholly in his element. He spoke very slowly and deliberately, enunciating carefully and choosing words with great precision. His voice was soft and high-pitched, with a distinct British inflection, and the extent of his vocabulary was astonishing, far larger than most of our own. This vocabulary extended not merely to the requirements of formal intellectual discourse, but also encompassed slang, aphorisms in foreign languages and neologisms in English. He always spoke extemporaneously and was always utterly cogent and lucid, no matter how frequently he refilled the sake glass. Most of us in this era took notes as he spoke, trying to focus intently on his words.

In any given talk, Rinpoche's discourse might range from formal exposition ("A person who is able to enter the buddhist path is someone who feels a sense of nonexistence, in whom some realization takes place so that struggle, neurosis, laziness, and aggression vanish—in the sense that there is no one to be angry or jealous. Ordinarily speaking this is not true, because we are full of all these emotions. Extraordinarily speaking, there is just space and energy, which do not need activating.

This is blue skyness, buddhanature, which has no characteristics in terms of conceptual labels. Theists accuse buddhism of nihilism, but this is positive nondiscovery") to invented language ("people who try to avoid the hard work of meditation are like cosmic hitchhikers") to contemporary idioms (new meditators might find themselves initially discouraged, because they are "speedy as hell, depressed as hell, fucked-up as hell.") Then in the question-and-answer period that always followed his talks, Rinpoche would display his brilliance and spontaneity further. ("Your speed comes from loneliness, ambition, jealousy. Slowing down your energy becomes lucrative. Slowing down is giving up.") All these remarks are from notes of a talk I attended in Boulder in December 1978.

But to reproduce Rinpoche's words is to unfurl only one aspect of the remarkable power of his presence. Buddhists believe the essential nature of every human being is *bodhichitta,* a Sanskrit word that translates as awakened mind or heart. Its natural expression is kindness or compassion. Trungpa Rinpoche was a veritable furnace of kindness; to be in his presence was to feel an elemental benevolent power that conferred a unique sense of privilege and obligation. This would be heightened for us, when, not infrequently, Rinpoche would linger at the end of the closing chants and say softly. "Please practice a lot. I love you all. A lot. You are extending my life" or some variant of these sentiments. Misty-eyed and with lumps in our throat, we would stand and bow as he took his final leave.

The Boulder community in this era was all-encompassing for me—it fulfilled all my needs, and I had little contact with people who were not members. It was primarily a spiritual community—we practiced and studied a lot—but there were also commercial, cultural and social dimensions. There was also a very active dating scene. During this era, I saw an article in a Denver alternative paper, written by a disaffected sangha member. She was particularly turned off by the extent to which the Boulder community felt to her like a meat market. It was a real fuck scene, she wrote bitterly. While I bridle at the reductiveness, it is tough to gainsay the claim. The Boulder community was indeed pretty promiscuous, as was my whole baby-boom generation. But as I conceded at the outset, the issue of our sexual behavior and the degree to which it mirrored Trungpa Rinpoche's behavior remain highly charged issues in the larger buddhist world, and may still be obstacles for potential students today. So let me describe my experience as a single guy during the heyday of Boulder buddhist scene.

We were a young adult community—in our late twenties and early thirties. Most of us accepted Rinpoche's view that the cultural norms of our society—work, marriage, family, among others—had an intrinsic wisdom and value that the hippie philosophy had denied. So those of us who were single and active in the dating scene were, consciously or not, in the market for a spouse. In such a context, sexual promiscuity is inevitable, even healthy. Within a few years I ended up married, as did almost everyone I knew, and became monogamous. In fact, so many people were marrying in Boulder in this era that you had to reserve the shrine room months and years in advance, and double and triple up on ceremonies (as my wife and I eventually did).

A different issue entirely (in my view) is how married people sometimes behaved. Rinpoche, of course, was married (although Diana, in this era, was around very little), and continually, publicly, had relationships with women who were his students. It is naïve to assume that this example did not implicitly sanction the practice of "open marriage," which was widespread in our sangha, although more so the further up the social scale the couple was situated. I'm quite conservative on this issue and did not practice open marriage. I am aware of some open marriages that have lasted over thirty years or more, but I know of very many more that have not. Of course, there were plenty of monogamous marriages that didn't make it either, but accommodating the repeated loss of focus that open marriage entails (or that I imagine it entails) must make weathering conflict extremely tough in the long run. There was a slippery assumption that the more "evolved" you were, the less you were fettered by attachment, lending the practice a bogus cachet. Personally I am not so evolved, and have not met many people who are—open marriage strikes me as a harmful form of entitlement. The fact that Rinpoche never advocated such behavior is beside the point. The reason we all drank sake, smoked cigarettes and wore conservative clothes is because *he* did. We emulated his behavior avidly, as people tend to do in communities with charismatic leaders. To this extent I believe that the example Trungpa Rinpoche set by his sexual behavior may have been harmful to some of his students. Perhaps paradoxically, I do not believe that Rinpoche's own behavior was an expression of entitlement. I will return to this subject at greater length later.

In late 1978 I finally straightened out my immigration status and was accorded permanent residency, allowing me to make my first trip back to England in nearly two years. Overall it was a bad experience. I was so concerned to convince my family and friends that I had not joined a cult that I came across as uptight and defensive. I saw Malcolm and Richard and other journalist friends in London (most had now graduated to the national media) and felt churlish and resentful in their company. My mother was in Scotland visiting her sister, and my father and I drove to-gether up to Glasgow, one of my all-time favorite places. However, I felt apologetic and tongue-tied in my aunt's flat, unable to explain what the hell I was doing so far away in such an unlikely community. On the way back to the south of England, I stopped in the Lake District to visit Tessa, who was now living in an unlikely community herself.

After I had visited Manjushri Institute, the traditional Tibetan dharma center in the north of England, Tessa made her own visit there later that summer. She never left and in fact is still a senior member of this community more than thirty years later. I had not realized before I left England the extent to which she was making an independent con-nection to dharma, which blossomed when she met the lamas in Cumbria. She and her boyfriend were living a short distance from the center; her best friend Brenda was also living nearby. Again it was strange and awkward. On some basic level I had not yet moved on and it was weird seeing her with another guy. Also while I was there I got re-ally sick—something about the combined cold and damp of the English winter wore me down. At Tessa's I came down with stomach flu so se-vere that I could barely make the bus trip back to London. I recuperated at my sister's house in North London, and then sold my remaining be-longings to buy my return flight to Denver, making my break with En-gland complete.

nine

One major development in our world during this era was Rinpoche's introduction of the Shambhala teachings, which led to a whole parallel path of training and practice. Trungpa Rinpoche "received" these teachings over a period of several years during the late 70s, which means he did not so much compose them as transcribe them from a spiritual source most of us cannot perceive. Later, the Tibetan texts were translated into English and became the basis of the array of Shambhala teachings that are still taught and practiced today.

The concept of Shambhala was not Rinpoche's invention—the legend of the kingdom of Shambhala (a Sanskrit word that is related to Shangri-La, first popularized by Victorian explorers) is widespread throughout Central Asia. It was believed to be an isolated kingdom where both the ruler and citizens were unusually enlightened. Indeed, the legend has it that when the historical Buddha visited, he found the culture so evolved that he taught the inhabitants the Kalachakra Tantra (Wheel of Time in Sanskrit), regarded as his highest of all his teachings. Trungpa Rinpoche's innovation was to codify the spiritual qualities of this society into a system of training that fostered their development without reference to any religious doctrine. Its basic practice was also sitting meditation, but its goal was not cessation of suffering through egolessness, as in the buddhist path, but the cultivation of warriorship, which Rinpoche characterized as a combination of gentleness and fearlessness.

Predictably, many of us scoffed when these teachings were first introduced while Rinpoche was still on retreat in 1977. I attended the first-ever Shambhala talk given in Boulder by David Rome, Rinpoche's private secretary, and his presentation of new concepts like "basic goodness" and "great eastern sun" was greeted by skeptical inquiries like "So what happened to suffering?" and "David, is this just buddhism lite?" But slowly, the Boulder community began to find the Shambhala teachings both challenging and inspiring. When Rinpoche came out of retreat, the program took a quantum leap forward, and after the texts he had written in retreat were translated, we began a graduate program to study them. Thirty years later, Shambhala training still flourishes on several continents and tens of thousands of people have been introduced to the practice of meditation through its unique, nondoctrinal approach.

Although I heard Rinpoche teach in many locations around Boulder during these years, the most treasured venue for me remained Rocky Mountain Dharma Center in the mountains north of Boulder. It was the site of my earliest connection to him, and seemed to be a place particularly dear to his heart. He had grown up in a mountainous, nomadic culture and the rugged terrain of RMDC seemed to make him especially happy. It was also a place where I was always very aware of my distinct neurotic style, but in a way that made it seem malleable, which felt both challenging and inspiring. I took every opportunity I could to practice there during the years I lived in Boulder.

The big summer program in 1979 was particularly memorable, and Rinpoche was in great form. The Shambhala training program was now well under way, and we had all become familiar with its prevailing esthetic, which stressed formality and elegance. After the first evening's talk, one student asked a question about how the elders of our lineage had expressed these same qualities. (He was probably thinking of its first two Tibetan forefathers, Marpa and Milarepa. Marpa was a working farmer and Milarepa, his student, was a wild yogi who spent decades in retreat, without bathing or cutting his hair. At one point he even turned green after subsisting for years on nettle soup.)

What, you think they were somewhat funky? Rinpoche responded, his shoulders shaking with mirth. Everyone laughed. Rinpoche then explained that these men were naturally elegant. Suits and dresses were merely a contemporary expression of the same inner wholesomeness they possessed.

Another student asked a question about the Dorje Kasung who were present. This was the second summer at RMDC at which Rinpoche had not stayed near the main tent in his usual trailer, but at a more distant encampment ground with a small group of guards. We did not see them during the day but they showed up for the evening talks, khaki-clad and jabbering into walkie-talkies. The officer who drove Rinpoche's Jeep even appeared to be packing a sidearm, to many people's consternation. Rinpoche was asked how carrying weapons jibed with the buddhist teaching of nonaggression.

Well, a moustache could be a weapon, he replied enigmatically to awkward laughter. Clearly people were uneasy about the kasung presence, and although still an active guard, I had no personal interest in these latest shenanigans, and felt almost embarrassed by them. In future years, Rinpoche adjusted the timing of these programs so the two did not coincide, and some years later my embarrassment would have its own particularly vivid fruition.

Later that summer the sangha travel business I worked for closed down after it ran out of seed money. The following day I came to the office to clean out my desk when the phone rang. To my surprise it was one of the directors of our sangha organization, calling me from Karmê-Chöling in Vermont to ask if I'd like to join the publicity department there. (He knew nothing about recent developments in my employment status.)

Are you free? he asked.

Actually, I am, I admitted.

So are you interested? he continued.

I asked a question about the stipend (miniscule, I learned), and accepted on the spot.

Karmê-Chöling is a white clapboard palace set in the rolling hills of northern Vermont. The original buildings and land had been bought by American students who had met Rinpoche in Scotland in the Sixties. Since then, new buildings had tripled its size to incorporate dormitories, a dining room and a magnificent meditation hall that blazed with gold leaf and satin. It felt like absolutely the right place for me to be in the fall of 1979, because I still had little ambition beyond my aspiration to understand dharma better, and happily accepted the three-year commitment to work in the center's PR department. In return I got to practice meditation four hours a day, to attend all its programs and to receive a stipend of ten dollars a week. It was perfect.

At the work meeting that began the new week I was introduced to the community and my new life. There were about fifty full-time residents, both staff and guests, including a lone monk from Texas. With the odd exception, everyone was in his or her twenties and thirties, white, middle class and college educated—an East coast version of the Boulder sangha. Naturally, I cast my single man's eye over the eligible females and noticed right away that a certain young woman called Mary clearly stood out. She was obviously highly respected among her peers, and I saw that she sat very straight when required to speak in public. (She was the administrative assistant to the two directors, so this happened almost daily.) Her demeanor was not, however, an affectation, but rather the reflection of a natural patrician grace. Unlike me, she was modest and reserved—her status in the community was clearly the result of personal merit, not ambition.

One distinctive feature of life in Trungpa Rinpoche's retreat community was the institution of "day-off." When I first learned of it at RMDC in 1976, I found the notion intriguing. An older student was explaining *dathun* to me (this is one of our signature programs, a month-long intensive sitting practice) and told me that there was traditionally a day off in the middle of the program on which there was no schedule and no requirements.

What do people do? I asked.

Party, he replied, laughing.

This appealed to me. The alternation of discipline and its absence, habitual behavior and highly regulated behavior, struck me as a way of understanding each more fully. And it was clear that the emphasis was on discipline, on renunciation. But the fact that you were not expected to renounce the gratification of sense appetites *entirely* struck me as both intelligent and realistic. We were lay people after all, and I for one had no aspiration to the rigors of monastic life. (When Rinpoche first announced the founding of Gampo Abbey, our monastic community in Cape Breton, Nova Scotia, I asked him anxiously at a community meeting whether enrollment would be voluntary. You wanna try some Kool-Aid? he responded mischievously.) I would likely have joined Trungpa Rinpoche's community whatever its requirements, but this tolerant (some might say indulgent) attitude toward sensual gratification made sense to me.

When the first day-off at Karmê-Chöling rolled around (actually, night-off and next-day-to-recuperate is more accurate), I'd made enough friends among the guys to make some modest plans—we would have a few drinks and then visit the local discotheque. I was actively wondering what Mary might be doing that evening, so I was thrilled when she and her girlfriends turned up after we'd been there for an hour or so. We danced and I bought her a drink and we spent the rest of the evening trying to chat over the deafening music. As the place closed I accepted a ride back in her friend's car, sitting next to her in the dark back seat, my heart pounding. On returning, she invited me to her room for a nightcap, and we were together for the next twenty-eight years. As I look back, Mary and I would likely have contrived to get together under any circumstances, but the accommodation of mating rituals within the Karmê-Chöling schedule certainly helped. The alternative is deceit and hypocrisy, qualities from which our sangha has largely been free.

Actually, falling in love with Mary was a tortured experience for me. What did that look mean? That slight hesitation? Was I being too presumptuous? Sometimes I would stay away for a day or more, feigning disinterest, because I sensed Mary's ambivalence. Other times I would thrill at my good fortune at meeting someone with her extraordinary qualities, who seemed to really like me, never wanting to leave the charmed intimacy of her room. Unlike my chronic hesitation with Tessa, I knew very quickly that I had met the person I wanted to marry. What was difficult was how to restrain my natural headlong style so as not to spook her completely. Mary was similar to Tessa in her intelligence, goodness and integrity. But she was different in a crucial way, in that she was not intimidated by me and stood her ground fearlessly. This was perhaps the decisive quality that convinced me of our relationship's viability, because I'd clearly met my match. Our romance blossomed through the fall and early winter, when both Rinpoche and the Regent came to visit.

Unlike the Boulder community with its thousand members, the Karmê-Chöling sangha would swell to maybe a couple of hundred when our teachers visited the center. In the run-up to the formal program, there were just a few dozen staff members in the house, and the sense of intimacy and connection was truly precious. The Karmê-Chöling living room is a large sunken space built straight into the hillside, and a giant granite boulder extends into the room. On their first evening, Rinpoche and the Regent took their seats in front of the rock to greet the community. We lined up to speak with one or both; I headed straight for the Regent. By this time I knew him fairly well, and I sought him out because he did not make me rigid with self-consciousness the way Rinpoche did.

What do you think about Mary and me? I asked.

He raised his eyebrows.

Okay, he said. But you've got to take her away from here.

I understood. Karmê-Chöling was too atypical an environment for the long-term prospects of any relationship formed there to be accurately gauged. What else we spoke of I no longer recall, because I had received the confirmation I was seeking. (I asked myself later how I might have reacted had he given me a more guarded response, which happened later with others making similar inquiries in my presence. In truth I would have been inclined to reconsider my feelings, which might seem shocking, but is nevertheless true. The fact is we routinely consulted both Rinpoche and the Regent over all manner of major personal decisions—where to live, whom to marry, what career to choose, etc. There was no separation between our personal and our spiritual lives, and seeking such advice was as natural as asking when and how to make a retreat, or how to work with a particular obstacle we'd encountered in meditation. If this proclivity made us a cult, well then we were and remained a cult during their lifetimes.)

Just how atypical this environment was became vividly clear to me several days later. Again, because of our relatively small numbers, I was scheduled to serve my first personal guard shift with Rinpoche during his visit. The personal guard typically accompanies Rinpoche from the residence to the talk, both driving his car and supporting him as he walks. I was both nervous and excited about this prospect, because the personal guard is directly responsible for the teacher's well-being and stays in close proximity to him throughout the shift. I showed up early in the morning to begin my shift long before Rinpoche and whoever his overnight guest might have been could be expected to emerge.

Rinpoche's residence in Vermont was a small, secluded house that had been purchased for his use a few miles' drive from the center. The guard's first task in the morning was to raise the flags on the poles on the front lawn (shades of my scouting days). I learned later that Rinpoche and his guest were awake, watching me from his bedroom window, joking about my peculiar, short overcoat and making puns on my name. There were further moments of comedy later when Rinpoche and his guest—who turned out to be one of my new friends at the center—came down to the kitchen in their robes to get tea, and it felt wonderful and natural to sit there with them both. This was my first direct encounter with the well-known fact that Trungpa Rinpoche slept with female students who were my peers. I had no feeling that his presence with his student/lover was transgressive—rather *my* inclusion gave me the sense of intimacy, appreciation and privilege. This sense of privilege was reinforced later that day when, after the evening talk at the main house, Rinpoche was chatting with folks in the main lobby as he prepared to leave. Suddenly he smiled and turned, then grabbed onto my left forearm without looking up at me, and we set off. It was such a gesture of trust that I got a lump in my throat, because I recognized that same gesture of trust characterized his whole presence among us.

It was during this visit that I learned from the Regent that I'd been accepted to Seminary later that year (he was speaking to the contents of the refrigerator at the time he told me. I was on guard duty again.) Seminary was our community's flagship program and competition for places was fierce. I had applied before leaving Boulder, but had not been accepted to the preliminary list of participants. However, everyone knew that dozens of places were held in reserve to be awarded later and somehow I had earned one of the coveted spots. I was elated and could not wait to tell Mary (she had attended the previous year). To explain why Seminary was such a big deal requires me to explain something of the uniqueness of Tibetan buddhism and how Trungpa Rinpoche chose to present its higher tantric or vajrayana teachings. ("Vajra" in Sanskrit, or "dorje" in Tibetan, denotes a small scepter used in ritual practices that represents a thunderbolt, and thus symbolizes indestructibility. Accordingly, vajrayana is sometimes translated as the Indestructible or Diamond Path.)

From its birthplace in Northern India in the sixth century BCE, buddhism spread first to China, Korea and eventually Japan, then centuries later north to Tibet then east to Mongolia. It also spread south and east to Sri Lanka, Burma, Thailand, Cambodia and Vietnam. The teachings of the historical Buddha were collected after his death into two major works of literature—the Pali and Sanskrit canons. The Pali canon forms the foundation of Southeast Asian buddhism and consists of scriptures known as *sutras*, a term which means teaching or instruction. The Sanskrit canon formed the basis of its northern expansion and includes both sutras and *tantras*, a term that means extension or continuity. Tantra predates buddhism and was practiced in the ancient Vedic religions of India. Because buddhism was eventually extirpated from the land of its origin following the Muslim invasions in the tenth century, the Tibetans became the primary custodians of the tantric tradition from the Middle Ages onwards. Lamentably, the terms tantra and tantric have been hopelessly misunderstood in modern Western culture, and are most frequently taken to refer to exotic sexual practices. To practitioners of buddhist tantra this is emphatically not what they mean.

Crudely, the sutric teachings of the Buddha explain the development of ego and the origin of suffering, and present the antidotes of egolessness and compassion, which lead gradually to *nirvana* or the cessation of suffering. The tantric teachings extend these same teachings to incorporate a variety of techniques that, if practiced skillfully, can accelerate this process dramatically. The most famous line of the Buddha's Heart Sutra says, "Form is emptiness, emptiness also is form." Sutric buddhism focuses on the first half of this formula, teaching with exquisite logic supported by the unshakeable confirmation of meditation practice that phenomena have no inherent nature other than that conferred by mind. Tantric buddhism accentuates the second half of the formula, that what is left when phenomena are perceived as empty is form manifesting as energy, which is irreducible, like space. This cosmic energy manifests in human life as emotional, perceptual, cognitive and behavioral patterns that can be the source of great suffering but also of great joy. Whereas the main practice of sutric buddhism consists of silent meditation on a simple object (the breath, part of the body, occasionally a text or an aspiration), tantric buddhism utilizes chanting, visualization, gesture, music and formless meditation to connect directly with confused energies and transmute them into their awakened, joyful state. The promise of these teachings was the main reason we were all so eager to be admitted to Seminary.

Unlike many Tibetan contemporaries, Trungpa Rinpoche did not believe his Western students were ready to receive the tantric teachings right away, without a major commitment to and demonstrated understanding of sutric buddhism. The danger, he explained, was that for people prone to spiritual materialism, the tantric teachings represented the ultimate ego trip and could backfire on us in a big way. For this reason, Rinpoche abstained from teaching tantra for his first three years in North America, stressing instead the discipline of sitting meditation and the teachings of emptiness. But in 1973, he resolved that a group of his students was ready for these higher teachings, which were introduced at a ten-week program that he called Seminary. The program had been held every year since (except the year he was on retreat) and was the major annual teaching event for our community, distinct from shorter, public programs. Seminary represented an intensive immersion in the complete buddhist canon presented by our extraordinary teacher, and culminated in a formal "transmission" or authorization to begin tantric practice afterwards. A lot of us secretly hoped that at Seminary we might finally "get it" and be catapulted forward in our development (despite the evidence that most Seminary graduates still seemed just like the rest of us). At very least we would take a big chunk of time out from our daily lives to devote ourselves to practice and study with Rinpoche. For these reasons I was truly overjoyed to be accepted.

Seminary in 1980 was held at Chateau Lake Louise, a sprawling resort hotel owned by the Canadian Pacific Railway Company and located in the Rockies near Banff, Alberta. It was undergoing renovation and was thus uninhabited except for a small work crew and us, three hundred or so buddhists from all over North America and Europe. I took the three-day train trip west from Montreal with a half-dozen or so other Karmê-Chöling staffers. Parting from Mary at Montreal station was a bittersweet experience; we pledged to write and call regularly and shared the conviction that our separation would not undo us.

Chateau Lake Louise was not unlike the forbidding, icebound hulk for which Jack Nicholson serves as caretaker in *The Shining*. Miles from other buildings up a steep, winding road, the hotel overlooked an exquisite glacial lake surrounded by soaring peaks. Everything was frozen and snowbound. Advance crews had converted the cavernous dining room into our shrine room and meditation hall; the lobby was our registration area, and the enormous industrial kitchen was set aside for our use. The participants occupied one half of the partially renovated structure, two to a room. Rinpoche, who arrived about a week after the event started, stayed in a suite that comprised several bedrooms, a study, dining room and kitchen.

By this stage the Seminary program had developed a distinct format. Ten days of sitting meditation would be followed by ten days of study and Rinpoche's presentation of the early sutric teachings, followed by a day off. Then ten days of sitting would be followed by ten days of study and teaching on the later sutras, followed again by a day off. Then after another sitting period, Rinpoche would introduce the vajrayana teachings and the program would conclude with the transmission ceremony for actual tantric practice. During the sitting periods alcohol was prohibited and all meals were eaten in meditation posture in the shrine room. During the study periods, drinking and socializing were permitted and dinners were eaten Western-style in one of the dining rooms. Thus the Seminary program was challenging but not austere. Unlike Japanese culture, Tibetan culture is fairly laid-back, and this difference is reflected in the contrasting styles of Zen and vajrayana. Intensive Zen practice usually begins very early, often five a.m., and the preferred meditation posture is extremely formal; even slight movement is discouraged. In certain Zen schools, meditators face a blank wall and a discipline master moves among them, sometimes slapping them on the shoulder with a *kyosaku*, a ceremonial staff, to sharpen their awareness. Our sitting style is formal but not militant—we are encouraged to shift position if our physical discomfort becomes distracting, and the more demanding meditation postures like the lotus and half-lotus positions are not encouraged. Meditation at Seminary began at seven a.m. and went until nine in the evening, with long breaks for lunch and dinner. The discipline master (*geko* in Tibetan) would circulate among us and offer a gentle touch if someone had actually fallen dead asleep or was leaning perilously one way or another. I like to think our approach includes more flexibility and sense of humor than the typical Zen style, although my personal experience of Zen practice is limited.

I loved Seminary from the start. Sitting along with three hundred or so others is very different than sitting in solitary retreat—you are still alone with your mind but you feel tremendous sangha support. There was a real sense of occasion, of doing something significant, and there were hordes of interesting people to meet and get to know. However, my sense of good fortune did not anticipate the development when Rinpoche's party finally arrived and John Perks summoned me up to the suite. Perks, in his trademark pinstripe suit and regimental tie, took me to one side and told me Rinpoche had chosen me as one of his *kusung* for the duration of the program. My first shift would be that night. I was speechless, but with hindsight I doubt Perks was telling me the whole truth. What is more likely is that Perks recommended a group of guards to serve as kusung for the program, and that Rinpoche signed off on his choices. Once again, the fact that I was English had probably helped considerably.

Kusung in Tibetan means "body protector," and the role was more personal and intimate than that of the anonymous vajra guard. The closest English equivalent would be valet, in that the kusung attended to the teacher's myriad personal needs throughout the day. For instance, because of his handicap, Rinpoche needed help with physical tasks like dressing and undressing, but the kusung also served hospitality to guests and controlled the flow of information between Rinpoche and the outside world. It was a multi-faceted role and I was very flattered to have been chosen; I was less thrilled by Perks' telling me that my first shift began later that day.

John, you're going to train me, right? The kusung is in charge of dinner service right? I don't know a thing about how to serve dinner, I explained.

Don't worry, said Perks. Come at five o'clock. Your shift begins at six.

I dutifully showed up in my best suit at the appointed hour. Perks was in the kitchen, and languidly offered me a glass of sake.

So how've you been, old chap? he asked, and we fell to chatting. Time passed and he introduced me to the other household staff as they showed up—the cook, the servers, the attaché (the person in charge of the daily schedule.) Eventually at six or so he led me into the formal sitting room where Rinpoche was seated wearing a cotton robe, chatting with guests. I bowed stiffly and took requests for drinks, which I managed to serve without major mishap. Perks remained in the kitchen, observing me mildly. I kept waiting for him to take me into the dining room for training, but nothing happened. Eventually, Perks went to speak to Rinpoche, then returned.

They're ready for dinner now, he explained. I've helped them get seated.

I was horrified.

Perks led me into the corridor and opened the door to the dining room.

Serve from the left and pick up from the right, he said, shoving me through the door and closing it behind me.

I had all the finesse that evening of a block of wood. I was paralyzed by my sense of ineptitude and intimidated by my sudden access to Rinpoche's inner world. Neither Rinpoche nor his guests seemed to mind my clumsiness, and somehow dinner got served and cleared away. Eventually the evening wound down and to my great relief Rinpoche was ready to turn in. I padded nervously behind him into his bedroom, eyeing the bow on the sash at the back of his robe. Somehow Rinpoche had to get out of that robe and into his bed and it was up to me to pull off the maneuver. I attacked the bow with gusto. It wouldn't give.

Rinpoche tried to say something to me over his shoulder but I ignored him, pulling at the bow. Trungpa Rinpoche was a stocky guy but soon I was yanking him round the bedroom like a sack of potatoes. He grabbed hold of the bedpost for purchase. Still I pulled and yanked and the bow would not give. He was trying to say something. I paused to listen.

It's a false bow, he said, pointing to the Velcro fastener at the side of the sash. I released the fastener and Rinpoche stepped out of his robe, relieved to be out of my clutches. Naked, he picked the sash off the floor and began trying to straighten the mangled bow on the bed with his good right hand. It was the closest he ever came to admonishing me. I was crimson with embarrassment, mortified by my inability to stop and listen to his simple instructions. I helped him into bed and muttered an apology, but he said goodnight in the sweetest way. I left and turned out the light.

The kitchen was empty so I poured myself a large glass of sake to steady my nerves. I was furious at Perks for his bogus "training" and furious at myself for being such a clown. I was not sure I could hack this kusung business—it was all too intense. The sudden introduction to Rinpoche's private world—the consorts, the prodigious drinking, the unpredictability—was disorienting to me. It was late. and I could not face returning to my room only to be rousted in a few hours for sitting practice, so I found a vacant bedroom in the suite, locked the door and went to sleep. Thus began my career as a shining star in the constellation of Trungpa Rinpoche's household.

The 16th Karmapa and Chögyam Trungpa, Rinpoche, circa 1962

Chögyam Trungpa, Rinpoche, circa 1982

With Tessa, Graduation Day at Cambridge, 1973

Rainbow upon arrival in Colorado, 1976

Congratulations from
the Vajra Regent, 1981

Allen Ginsberg visits my classroom in Denver, 1982

Flags and lhasang hearth, Encampment Grounds, 1984

Tea and rice ceremony with Jamgon Kongtrul, Rinpoche, 1985

Strolling with Jamgon Kongtrul, Rinpoche and monks, 1985

Final kusung shift at the
cremation ceremony, 1987

ten

After the mortification of that first kusung shift with Trungpa Rinpoche, I resolved to face down my squeamishness and make the most of this privileged opportunity I had been given. In truth, it appealed to my ambition to make my mark in Rinpoche's world and be of service to him. I was also aware that for the first time that as a kusung, I had some modest status in our community.

An important step was to become less ham-fisted. On my next shift I had the crucial insight that it was stupid for me to try and be invisible around him—that only made me more self-conscious. A better idea was to be natural and not feel like it was a problem that I was in his space— I had a function that was both welcome and necessary. Thus I began to feel more attentive to the quality of the energy around him and adjust my behavior accordingly. Some days were spent in study—Rinpoche based many of his talks at the 1980 Seminary on texts by Lodrö Thaye, the great nineteenth-century scholar known as Jamgön Kongtrul the Great—and meeting with senior students who were teaching other classes at Seminary. At these gatherings, I would bring Rinpoche writing materials and serve everyone water. On other occasions there would be parties with impromptu performances of music and dance. At such gatherings I would serve drinks and might stay and watch, without actually participating. I learned to anticipate Rinpoche's needs and to exchange repartee with him. We teased each other about whether Oxford or Cambridge University was superior, and would trade private jokes about English culture. I began to lean deliberately into my Englishness, and cultivated a certain Jeeves demeanor. (After taking his little dog Yumtso out for a walk, I would report, "Nothing was forthcoming, sir," which would make him laugh. John Perks, of course, *was* Jeeves, thus did not need to contrive his behavior at all.) Very quickly I felt comfortable and relaxed around Rinpoche, which was a precious legacy of my service to his household. Many students remained so awestruck by him they were completely helpless and tongue-tied in actual encounters.

One particular shift became my favorite. Because there were several hundred participants at Seminary, Rinpoche rarely granted personal interviews. However, students could and did sign up for group interviews of fifteen or so. Rinpoche would hold these gatherings at different places around the cavernous hotel, and I would be responsible for bringing along the sake and the Kleenex (Rinpoche always had to remind me. Like any practiced therapist, he knew to anticipate tears.) Then, of course, I got to be present as he responded to the myriad concerns of his students—with spouses and children, livelihood, spiritual doubt, beefs with the hierarchy, whatever. He had absolutely no agenda at these meetings; he listened carefully and responded directly to the real issue behind each question. His ability to communicate with diverse people in the most appropriate and helpful way was truly extraordinary. The tantric tradition calls this joining of wisdom and compassion skillful means. Trungpa Rinpoche was the embodiment of skillful means.

Seminary was the annual occasion at which Trungpa Rinpoche liked to showcase innovation, and the 1980 event was no exception. The previous year he had introduced *lojong,* a tradition of contemplation using slogans devised by the Indian master Atisha. In 1980 he taught further on lojong but also on *tonglen,* a practice that embraces the suffering of others and extends compassion in return. There were also new rituals, including *oryoki,* a formal style of eating from the Zen tradition, a new processional entry before talks, also from Zen, and drumming accompaniment to chanting, common to both the Tibetan and Zen traditions. Oryoki requires dexterity with two hands, and was taught by his students; the procedures for the processional and for drumming he taught us himself. There were further Japanese innovations introduced at this Seminary, reinforcing the dominant Zen style of our community's culture and practice, which it retains to this day.

The night before the second *sutrayana* sitting period began I was on kusung duty with Rinpoche when he asked me to summon a particular participant, a woman I knew from Boulder who was one of his regular girlfriends. I thought this was probably just a date, except Rinpoche in-structed me to have her bring her scissors. When she arrived, Rinpoche had me set him up on a stool in one of the bathrooms and asked her to cut his hair. He kept telling her to cut it shorter and shorter until his head looked something like a scraped turnip. Then I was dispatched for shaving cream and a razor and together they shaved him completely bald, leaving his skull shiny and blood-spattered. By now it was some eleven years since Rinpoche had renounced monasticism, and he had al-ways worn his hair thick and shaggy. To see him with a monk's shaved scalp was truly startling. However, there were more surprises in store the next day.

As sitting resumed after breakfast at nine o'clock, Rinpoche arrived with glistening scalp and wearing a resplendent canary robe and golden *rakusu*, a ceremonial teaching bib given to him by Maezumi Roshi, the Zen master from Los Angeles. He took his seat on a cushion next to the shrine, facing us—the first time in my experience that he had led a meditation session for us. For the next three hours he sat like a rock, completely motionless, as we sat and walked, sat and walked in front of him. Until this point, Rinpoche typically appeared in public in dark business suits, and his thick black hair was a distinctive feature. Many Seminarians had no clue as to who he was, and thought some visiting Zen master had shown up to lead the morning sitting. Rinpoche kept his head shaved for the next several years, and began to favor formal robes over business suits from this time on.

The night before the first day-off I was on duty with Rinpoche again and really hoped he would opt for an early night, because I thought I might be able to catch one of the many parties scheduled that night. No such luck—Rinpoche had a full house of guests who stayed until after midnight. Then when the suite finally cleared out he sum-moned the personal guard and me to help him with a construction project in preparation for the next day. He had decided on a foray onto frozen Lake Louise, and needed a conveyance to get him there. To this end he had acquired a couple of toboggans and a lawn chair and it was our job to figure out how to lash all three together to fashion a sort of sedan-chair sled. We had rope but no tools and were frankly stymied by the task. Rinpoche, however, was not. The three of us sat cross-legged on the floor of the living room while he gave instructions on how to tie the toboggans together and then secure the lawn chair on top. All the while we drank sake and told jokes. Rinpoche particularly liked jokes about the Gelugpas (whose name means "Virtuous Ones"), the traditional Tibetan rivals of his own, less conservative sect. In one joke the Gelugpas were po-faced monks who nevertheless got erections when they hiked their robes to cross a river and saw pretty girls on the other side. He took childish delight in his naughty stories and his shoulders shook with laughter. Any frustration I had with my missed social opportunities had long ago evaporated. We test-drove the sled up and down the corridor of the suite and then called it a night. I helped Rinpoche to bed and turned in sometime around four.

I woke too late the next morning to join in any of the organized activities—there were trips scheduled to the ski slopes, the hotels in Banff, the stores in Calgary—I had missed them all. Our hotel seemed completely deserted and I started to mope, wondering what on earth I could find to do beside my laundry. I remembered Rinpoche's lake trip and wandered up to the suite. Half a dozen people, mostly guards, were making preparations for the excursion, and Rinpoche was calling the shots, from the composition of the sandwiches ("Heavy on the fat, for me") to the proportions of rum, hot water and lemon juice in the thermos he was planning to bring along. I retrieved my outdoor gear and joined the crew down at the frozen lake. Some wore Alpine skis and others were on foot, taking turns pulling the sled over the packed snow. Rinpoche sat like a Mongolian pasha in his lawn chair, a fur hat on his head, a plaid blanket around his knees, and a huge grin in his face. It was bitterly cold but he was in great form and his enthusiasm was infectious. A couple of times the sled tipped over and dumped him in the snow; he would lie there laughing until we hauled him upright into his chair again. Eventually we got to the end of the lake where we stopped for our picnic. Rinpoche passed around the plastic cup of rum and looked across at an almost vertical mountain pass opposite us.

How long to climb that? he asked.

At least a day, someone said.

No, three hours, Rinpoche corrected.

How? The snow's way too deep, someone else said.

Rinpoche explained that you send someone ahead to lie in the snow to press it down so you all can walk over the surface. The "pressers" take turns because the task is so exhausting. We realized then he was talking from experience, from leading his followers across the Himalayas into India when he was nineteen, and we all fell silent at the thought.

Who's got the rum? he asked, breaking the mood, and we set off back.

It was a magical day and I returned to my room much more inspired than if I'd eaten restaurant food or visited the tourist sites of Banff. Seminary was like that for me, full of unexpected, and from my point of view then, undeserved privileges.

There was a universal assumption that participants at Seminary would have flings, whether they were married or not. In due course I connected with someone I knew from Boulder, a married woman I had considered too exotic to be interested in an oafish fellow like me, and we maintained a light and affectionate connection for the rest of the program. Nervously, during my next phone call with Mary, I told her I had slept with someone, giving her the person's name, although I knew she did not know her.

She in turn told me she'd slept with a guy I knew at Karmê-Chöling.

My blood turned to ice. Oh, that's cool, I managed.

He's good to talk to, she said.

I quickly changed the subject and we spoke of I remember not what.

Back in my room I experienced rage and panic. Good to talk to? Good to talk to, huh? Well, that's it, we're through. She obviously prefers him. I sought consolation with my roommate, our mutual friend Johnny Walker and eventually (although this bit is hazy) a woman from Los Angeles who lived next door. And next morning I was back on my cushion, seeing the transparency of my thoughts, resting my mind on the outbreath.

Of course, I'm aware of certain contradictions here. In my first mention of sexual behavior in our sangha, I climbed aboard the high horse of sanctimony to denounce the practice of open marriage. Yet, after having begun my first committed relationship since arriving in America, here I was at Seminary having an affair with a married woman. And I notice I've chosen terms like "fling" and "light and affectionate" in what is doubtless a deliberate attempt to minimize my behavior and its repercussions. (The woman in question and her husband did ultimately divorce, as did Mary and I, decades later.) And while I pretended nonchalance at Mary's similar confession, I was in fact bitterly jealous and somewhat scared.

My defense sounds like a catalog of rationalization and hypocrisy. First and foremost, Seminary was different. It wasn't real life—it was a heightened interlude from real life. Everyone, and I mean *everyone*— old, short, tall, gay, straight—was in the dating game. It was toughest for those who came as couples, married or not; for many I knew, the pressure broke them up. There was a strong sense of discipline at Seminary, but also of celebration, almost of festival. Our sexual behavior reflected this assumption that "normal rules" were suspended.

In truth, there was also a sense of entitlement (precisely what I criticize in the practice of open marriage.) We knew we were being schooled in a profound system of spiritual training, and we believed we were somehow special because of this, and so we felt entitled to indulge ourselves while we were about it. In this again, we had the example of our teacher, who reveled in the field of the senses as completely as in the vast and fathomless doctrine that he was unveiling for us. It did not feel in the least problematic to me at the time, or contradictory, although now my conduct strikes me as immature and somewhat irresponsible. And as events ultimately unfolded in our sangha, the issue of sexual irresponsibility would have the most catastrophic consequences for us.

eleven

At the 1980 Seminary, Trungpa Rinpoche gave twenty-six talks over an eleven-week period, covering a huge span of buddhist dharma. Each talk was followed by an extensive question-and-answer period. During his life he led thirteen Seminaries and gave more than three hundred talks. Many cover the same topics, but each talk is utterly distinct. The collected Seminary transcripts are currently being edited and will constitute an encyclopedia of buddhism when published.

One event during the final stage of Seminary stands out for me. Typically, the Vajra Regent Ösel Tendzin visited toward the end of the program to join in our activities. In 1980 he was in retreat and so sent a letter to be read to the community in his stead, which turned out to be a personal narrative of his own connection to Trungpa Rinpoche and how he became his dharma successor. The letter explained how in 1971 he was known as Narayana and living in Los Angeles as a member of the Integral Yoga Institute led by the Hindu teacher Swami Satchidananda. In February of that year he was dispatched to Boulder to invite Trungpa Rinpoche to a "world enlightenment festival" in California. Narayana met Rinpoche for the first time at his home outside Boulder, and was very unsettled by the encounter, particularly by the bottle of Scotch on the table throughout the interview. When he returned the following month for a longer visit, he asked Rinpoche directly why he drank (as a Hindu, Narayana was both vegetarian and a nondrinker).

Sometimes it is necessary to insult in order to communicate, was Rinpoche's response.

Soon after, Narayana and his best friend and their wives left the IYI to become Rinpoche's students. They moved to the village of Kirby, Vermont, close to Karmê-Chöling, and started a bakery. In September of

1971 Rinpoche unexpectedly told Narayana that he wanted him to become his Gampopa (Gampopa was the dharma successor of the great
yogi Milarepa and founder of the monastic order of Rinpoche's lineage).
He told him he did not expect to live a long life and needed to identify
and train a successor. On the spot, Narayana accepted, although his new
status was not revealed to our community for another five years. The
Regent's letter explained how when Rinpoche finally made the appointment public to a gathering of staff in April 1976, the reaction among his
peers ranged from elation to depression, emphasizing how outrageous
the appointment really was. No Westerner had yet been appointed successor to a Tibetan buddhist teacher. Narayana, formerly Tom Rich, an
Italian-American from suburban New Jersey, had no unusual pedigree
that distinguished him from anyone else. He was in fact one of us—a
former hippie and spiritual seeker, confused, ambitious and hedonistic, a
quintessentially American product of the Sixties. While this appointment would become particularly contentious after Rinpoche's death, at
the 1980 Seminary Ösel Tendzin still enjoyed wide support and inspired
deep devotion within our sangha.

I returned from Seminary in May 1980 to a loving reunion with Mary
in Montreal and soon after with our friends at Karmê-Chöling. I felt
buoyant and relaxed and ready for the next stage of life, which was certain to unfold somewhere other than Karmê-Chöling. Mary and I decided to get married soon after my return. She too felt ready for the
next stage—she was overripe to leave, having already lived at the center
for more than three years. First, however, we had to help staff a big
event celebrating the tenth anniversary of the founding of Karmê-
Chöling. Rinpoche and his wife Diana, whom I had never met, were
scheduled to preside over the celebration in a large meadow high above
the main house.

Mary and I were well into the throes of these preparations when
Rinpoche and Diana arrived, and were surprised when the next day we
were summoned to meet them. We duly changed into respectable
clothes and went up to the suite where they were waiting for us in
Rinpoche's sitting room. Diana, gracious and animated, did most of the
talking; Rinpoche, bald and inscrutable, listened mildly. It turned out

Diana had a problem with one of her horses, Shambhala, as he had developed an intestinal parasite and was now stranded in England. She had recently decided to return to the States after studying dressage in Europe for several years but had been obliged to leave both her horses behind, along with a sangha couple who had been her attendants in Austria and England. This couple was now bored and lonely and knew little of equine matters. Somehow, Diana had learned that Mary had owned horses in her teens. Would we like to go England for a few months, relieve her personal attendants of their supervision of Shambhala's veterinary care, and then arrange for his shipment back to America? We could join the household on the grounds of a stately home in Warwickshire, and receive room and board. Did we need time to think about it? Well, no we didn't. We accepted on the spot, in large part because the offer conformed magically to our own developing plans. We'd already decided to leave Karmê-Chöling and needed to introduce Mary to my family in England before we got married. We were also flattered to be invited to undertake such a personal mission for our teacher's wife. Diana was warm and appreciative and Rinpoche beamed his approval.

We left for England soon after the anniversary event, a memorable evening that featured a string quartet, an impromptu striptease by a lady from Texas, and copious speeches and toasts. It also featured me as Master of Ceremonies, again because in this era I retained the strong English accent Rinpoche favored. After the Texan stripper was carefully escorted from the immediate vicinity by two khaki-clad vajra guards (an intervention that entered kasung lore as The Yellow Rose Incident), I scribbled a note on my program and passed it up to Rinpoche. "What do you get when you cross a quintet with a naked girl?" I quipped. "Answer: a sextet." Rinpoche read, chortled, scribbled something himself and handed it back. "Contrapuntal," he wrote beneath the joke. I was not sure what the word meant, but Rinpoche clearly did and was pleased with his witticism, offering me a mock bow of acknowledgement. His main personal contribution to the entertainment was trapping June bugs in his mouth (they are a sort of giant flying cockroach), then turning to someone on the high table, opening his mouth and letting the insect crawl out and fly away.

Over the years I had learned to expect bizarre developments in Trungpa Rinpoche's world, but it was nevertheless tough to explain to my family and friends exactly how we came to be living in the deerkeeper's lodge of Lord Leigh's estate in Warwickshire, supervising the care of a dressage horse worth tens of thousands of pounds. The lodge was a tastefully converted seventeenth-century house set in acres of grounds leading down to the River Avon. In the bucolic distance was Lord Leigh's mansion, like the backdrop for a period TV drama. The two dressage horses were stabled ten miles away in Stratford, and once we had visited them and checked in with the vet, there really was not a whole lot for us to do beyond watch reruns of "Dallas" on the television and get going on our prostrations, an activity that needs some explanation.

Prostrations are one of the four *ngöndro* practices (pronounced NUN-dro in Tibetan), which are preliminary practices undertaken before beginning an actual tantric deity practice. In the distant past, students who requested initiation into a particular tantric ritual were required to demonstrate their devotion by undergoing all manner of hardship and tests. Famous examples include Naropa, who underwent all kinds of mortification at the hands of his teacher Tilopa, and Milarepa, whose teacher Marpa made him build and tear down a stone tower multiple times before granting him the initiation he sought. (The tower stood from the twelfth century until 1966, when some Chinese Red Guards blew it up.) Some time later this test of devotion and commitment was formalized into the four ngöndro or preliminary practices, which most students of Tibetan buddhism are required to complete. Flat-out the practices might take you six months; most Western students take several years to complete them; many never finish at all. The consensus is that the most difficult of the four is the first, which consists of 108,000 full-body prostrations.

An excellent description of the ngöndro practices can be found in Stephen Butterfield's 1994 memoir *A Double Mirror*. Like most tantric practice, prostrations include a visualization, a mantra recitation, and physical gestures, although in this case the gesture entails the unlikely act of throwing yourself full-length on the floor, touching your forehead and extending your hands toward the shrine, then standing up again (and counting off one bead on your *mala* or rosary). We had learned to facilitate the practice by wearing cut-off socks on our hands, pads on our knees, and utilizing Masonite prostration boards to allow for easier sliding. Even so it was a grueling practice that wore you out after a few hundred repetitions. The four of us practiced in the makeshift shrineroom/gym above the garage where we would flail, grunt and sweat together for several hours each morning. This peculiar ritual was naturally something we chose not to discuss with our occasional visitors.

The summer was chilly and wet. Shambhala the horse made slow but measurable progress, and mostly we looked forward to our weekend visitors. We saw most of my closest friends and many of my relatives over the course of the summer. As Shambhala was on schedule to recover and be shipped back to the States in September, Mary and I began to consider where we might live on our return. Boston had been an early choice because it was close to Karmê-Chöling, but neither of us felt really drawn to the place. Mary preferred New York City, where she'd lived after college, but we couldn't see moving there without jobs or a place to live. One place that was definitely out was Boulder—Mary didn't like the competitive social scene and I knew it would be a tough place to make a living. All in all, a big city seemed like a better bet. Eventually we settled on Montreal, a place that held fond memories for us both and to which I might be able to emigrate relatively easily as a British citizen. We made an appointment to visit the Canadian consulate in Birmingham when late one night the phone rang. It was Rinpoche calling for me.

I had not taken a personal call from Rinpoche before and so took the phone with some trepidation. His request was straightforward. His teenage son Gesar had returned to Boulder from Europe with his mother and needed a personal tutor to supervise his education. Rinpoche favored the British education system. Would I move to Boulder and tutor Gesar in the equivalent of the British A Level curriculum? I could pick up the necessary books in London before I came back. We could live at Marpa House, our sangha boarding house. I was tongue-tied and asked for a moment to relay the request to Mary, who was sitting next to me in mounting alarm. I told Rinpoche I was very flattered but needed time to think about it. We were planning to get married and were unsure how such an arrangement would fit into our plans. He told me to take all the time we needed. We would talk again in a week or so.

Mary needed no such interval to make up her mind. No way, she said, after I hung up. I just lived with fifty other people for three years. I can't live at Marpa House. It would drive me nuts.

I could see her point. Neither was I convinced that tutoring Gesar Mukpo, a young man with an erratic school history, was a job for which I was particularly suited. But the invitation was clear—to convert our temporary status as members of Rinpoche's household into something more permanent. What sangha members in general craved was access to Rinpoche, and here it was being offered to us in spades. Again, of course, I was flattered. But I was also deeply equivocal.

Next day the lobbying from Boulder began. Two members of the board called to repeat the terms of the offer and pitch it as a test of my devotion. I was genuinely torn, because I could not imagine turning Rinpoche down flat (and it was Rinpoche who had asked me after all, not Diana) but to accept seemed grossly unfair to Mary and harmful to our prospects. We stewed for a few days then left for London, where the Regent was due to visit on the last leg of a European tour. He was scheduled to lead a community meeting and a shrine blessing at a new center in South London, close to where I used to live with Tessa.

The Regent knew us both fairly well and when he saw that we were agitated, he ushered us into the sunny backyard of the house before the community event began. We explained our predicament and the Regent asked me simply, Does it click?

No, I answered truthfully.

Then don't do it.

You never said no to Rinpoche, I objected.

Well, what he asked me always clicked. So I never had to, he said.

This made me feel better. So just turn it down? I probed.

You could, he said.

Not for the last time, the Regent's words were balm to my agitated soul.

I looked at Mary. She seemed considerably relieved.

I was still uneasy, however, and on our way back to Warwickshire we hatched a compromise, which entailed Mary reluctantly agreeing to move to Boulder. I would offer to work with Gesar part-time but we would find our own place to live and get jobs to support ourselves. We called Rinpoche with the offer and he said he was happy for whatever help I could offer—we should come on out to Colorado. Within a couple of weeks Shambhala's blood test was clear, and we escorted him overnight to a cargo hangar at Heathrow. Within another couple of weeks we were back in Boulder, having arranged to rent a couple of rooms in a sangha household. My new life as an aspiring husband and part-time tutor was about to begin. Except that it wasn't.

Some time during the next week I made my way over to Kalapa Court for my first meeting with Gesar. I waited in the small sitting room near the front door and eventually Diana came down the stairs to talk to me. Her face was stern. She explained that since I could not make a full-time commitment, my services would not be needed. Gesar needed a full-time tutor, and she had already made other arrangements. Objections crowded my mind but I was too shocked to speak. I assented politely and left.

Unsurprisingly Mary was not thrilled to learn that we had moved to Boulder on a false pretext, but we had to make the best of it. The singles playground of Boulder suddenly looked very different from my new perspective as future husband and breadwinner. We bought a rusted VW hatchback that leaked exhaust into the cab and found minimum-wage jobs. Inevitably, our first winter in Boulder was somewhat tense.

All was not bleak, however. We were both active in community events and began to make new friends among couples who were at a stage of life similar to our own. Unexpectedly, the Regent invited me to become one his regular kusung (my permanent appointment to the kusung division had been confirmed at Seminary). I accepted gratefully, both because of my admiration for him and because there was little chance of getting onto Rinpoche's schedule in Boulder unless a kusung actually expired. I thus became the Regent's regular kusung for Saturday evening, which practically guaranteed late nights and far-flung social events, unless he was physically sick or out of town. I worked with him for three years in this way until I left Boulder for the second time, and was fortunate to develop an extremely close bond with him.

By now the kusung role felt very natural to me. It was less formal than the uniformed kasung role, and allowed me to serve and support the teacher's activity in a way that was intimate and gratifying. The Regent had no physical handicap—far from it—and needed no help with routine physical tasks. But he did appreciate my support in countless other ways in formal and informal settings, and I felt grateful for his confidence in me. He was not beyond speaking sharply if I did something clumsy or foolish, but in general he treated me with great kindness and affection and referred to me often as "Tunnuch," a pet name his family had given to an uncle also called Tony. Saturday night would often find us at gatherings large and small; alcohol was omnipresent at these events, and he would often be worse for wear by the time the evening ended. I enjoyed the responsibility of getting him home safely, supporting him as he got undressed and into bed, filling the pitcher of ice water and the whispering humidifier, my final tasks before I took my leave.

As I got to know him better, it became clearer why Trungpa Rinpoche had chosen him as his successor. He was a charismatic man, charming, funny and big-hearted. He was talented and courageous. He was also a brilliant dharma teacher and made strong, intuitive connections with people in the same way Rinpoche did. And he was devoted to Rinpoche as no one else, with every cell of his being, and had completely given up his life to serve him. Of course, as second-in-command to Rinpoche, he also enjoyed considerable power and perquisites, and some people resented this. I did not. As I got to know him better I learned that he was occasionally given to bombast, cronyism and self-indulgence, but I grew to love him ardently and trust him implicitly. He might occasionally be mean to people—including me—in a bantering way (I have the same tendency), but I knew that on a deeper level I could count on him absolutely, and most people I knew felt the same way. We were proud of him because he discharged his difficult role so superbly. His brilliance reflected on us and I could not imagine any other of Rinpoche's students in his place. I looked forward to my Saturday evenings in his service as a privilege.

By now the Regent's family had moved to their own large house in Boulder a few blocks from the Kalapa Court. Like Rinpoche, the Regent frequently had overnight guests other than his wife (the widely adored

Lila, whom we all referred to as Lady Rich), although in the Regent's case the guests could be of either sex. At the time I was not judgmental about these liaisons; they always seemed consensual and were none of my business. As I've explained, open marriage was not unusual in our community.

After six months in Boulder, Mary's and my situation began to improve. We both found work in Denver, enduring the hour-long commute each way in our malodorous hatchback. We rented a new house with some married friends. I did not have much contact with Rinpoche's household in this era, but I felt awkward if I ran into Diana at social events. But then, around this time I was invited to work with his family again. Rinpoche's eldest son Ösel, whom we all called the Sawang (the title means "earth lord" in Tibetan) was in his late teens and also received private tutoring. The woman who oversaw his education asked me whether I'd like to get involved as a writing tutor, and I tentatively agreed. However, I was apprehensive about such a role given my abortive experience with Gesar, and also unsure about tutoring a young man whom I considered a friend. I'd made an early connection with Ösel Mukpo when I first moved to Boulder in my mid-twenties and he was fifteen. I took him on a camping and rafting trip and would often play soccer with him and his teenage friends, both young men and women, in North Boulder Park. But the plan encountered a persistent scheduling problem and eventually the tutorial idea lapsed, to our mutual relief. Twenty-five years later, Ösel Mukpo, now recognized as the tulku Sakyong Mipham Rinpoche, is head of Shambhala International and is the author of several beautifully written books, so our lost opportunity clearly did him no permanent harm.

Mary and I were married in the community shrine room by Ösel Tendzin in June 1981, along with two other couples. Mary's parents and siblings attended, mine did not, because of the distance and expense. It was a splendid day, and we convened our reception in the balmy evening in the spacious yard of a friend's house. The Regent was in fine form, giving a short, lucid talk on meditation during the ceremony and charming the relatives and guests at the reception. Allen Ginsberg was among those present; Rinpoche was expected, but fell ill the day before and was unable to attend. We were a little apprehensive how Mary's parents, from stern Protestant stock, might respond to the somewhat gaudy style that the Boulder sangha affected, but they were genuinely delighted that we had so many friends and impressed by our "minister" the Regent. My father-in-law gave a speech in which he thanked him for "formalizing a relationship that has existed for some time." Everyone laughed. We felt relieved and grateful to the Regent for being such a consummate pro, a front man you could count on to represent everything that was best in our community.

twelve

My parents, Norman and Catherine, met at the end of World War II at a dance hall on Sauchiehall Street in Glasgow, where my mother lived with her sister and where my father's father, a Methodist preacher from the north of England, had been posted by his church. My father, a witty after-dinner speaker, later described their actual meeting thus: "I spied this attractive piece across the dance floor and when the band struck up a tango, I approached and asked her to dance. She said, 'I don't know the tango.' I said, 'Neither do I.' Those were the first two lies we told each other."

Norman Cape had by this time been in uniform for six years and was due to be reassigned to the occupation forces in Germany. He had spent the war years as a dispatch rider in East Africa, India and Burma and was by now sick of army life. He learned that if he were married, his assignment would be vacated and he could accelerate his demobilization. Thus my parents were married in October 1945.

High-speed courtship and marriage were not rare in this era as those lucky enough to survive World War II set about creating lives of predictability and safety. Marriage and steady work were the avenues to this common goal. Both my parents had grown up in homes that valued education, although neither benefited much in a formal sense. My Dad left school at fourteen after his own father went bankrupt during the Depression. My mother left school and home at age sixteen to escape an abusive father and moved in with her elder sister, who was living a bohemian lifestyle among artists and radicals in Glasgow. Her sister's husband Jack, my beloved boyhood mentor, was an anti-war activist, a "conshie" who was jailed in the forties for resisting the draft. He was also an artist, musician and spiritual seeker who meditated and studied

Eastern religion. My mother worked in Glasgow as a secretary and typist before meeting my father at the end of the war.

My mother was always psychologically frail, scarred by a childhood of neglect and abuse. But she was what her first psychiatrist deemed "well compensated" for most of her adult life, raising three children and running a firm but loving household. She derived strength and meaning from the task of motherhood and my sisters and I do not recall any big crises until my father told her he wanted to separate when I was at college. They lived apart for almost a year but were eventually reconciled, moving to the south of England a few years later when my father retired. However, they made a lousy choice of a place to live—an Elizabethan thatched cottage in a tiny village with no bus service and a fifteen-minute drive to the nearest shop. My mother, who had been a city-dweller her whole life, who did not drive, was suddenly stranded in the middle of nowhere, dependent on my father for her every move. He was absolutely fine—a stamp collector and aspiring writer, he shut himself away in his study. But my mother became more and more isolated and depressed, to the extent that my father agreed to relocate to the nearby town where she could have more mobility. But well before they could pull off their move, my mother had become paralyzed by depression, bed-ridden and unresponsive. Her local GP tried a succession of medications to no avail, and by the time they moved to their small, modern house in town the doctor had switched her to Parnate, an older medication that came with a host of dietary restrictions. Unfamiliar with these, my mother ate something to which she had a violent, psychotic reaction. Cowering in her bed, she hallucinated that the cat entering the room was a giant rat coming to attack her. To escape the creature she opened the window and leapt fifteen feet onto a paved patio, breaking an ankle and damaging vertebrae. She lay there injured and delusional until the ambulance took her to the hospital in Cambridge. By the time her injuries were treated, she had become convinced that she herself had turned into a rat with a giant, hairless tail. Eventually she was taken from there to Fulbourn Hospital, a mental hospital nearby with a fearsome reputation among Cambridge University students.

I learned all these details on the telephone from my elder sister in the spring of 1982 while sitting in the principal's office at the private school where I worked in Denver. Both my sisters had young kids and were unable to support my father, who was distraught and alone. Mary and I left immediately and moved in with him, caring for him and visiting my mother almost every day. I was very suspicious of the hospital psychiatrist and his regimen, demanding to know the names of the drugs he was giving my mother (a carelessly prescribed drug had been responsible for her psychotic break, after all) and arguing that she ought to be in intensive psychotherapy to work on her "issues." The psychiatrist, a scruffy fellow with a pronounced nervous tic, explained that the best treatment for her would be ECT (electro convulsive therapy, which my mother would eventually receive multiple times), but was not allowable because of her spinal injuries. The alternative was drug therapy, which would take longer. However, I remained as combative as I was ill informed. Somehow I imagined my poor, damaged mother reliving her childhood trauma in order to transcend it, whereas she barely had the ego-strength to support our visits. It was wrenching to see her so bewildered and sick, but at least the nursing staff seemed kind and attentive and there was no realistic alternative. When we left after three weeks my mother showed no improvement, and I was unsure whether she would ever live outside an institution again. As it transpired, my mother eventually recovered and was discharged, but experienced multiple relapses and many more hospitalizations before her death in 1997. Amazingly, I made no connection between her illness and my own experience of depression after Belfast, which I think I had categorized as a freak, one-time occurrence. When I came to write my first novel five years later, my experiences at Fulbourn Hospital provided the basis for several of the scenes I wrote.

After three years in Boulder, Mary and I were barely making a living and decided it was time to move. I had landed in nonprofit business management and in the spring of 1983 we took a trip to New England where I interviewed for several business manager positions at independent schools. I was relatively young and inexperienced and could not quite convince the people I met that I was the right man for the job. Then I was unexpectedly invited to New York to interview at Brooklyn Friends School, a position that had not been advertised when I made my initial trip. The school was in downtown Brooklyn in a gloomy art-deco fortress that had once housed the Brooklyn Law School. This time I hit it off with the principal ad trustees immediately. The Quakers have the closest affinity to buddhism of any Christian sect (their basic form of worship is communal silence), and I seemed to ask all the right questions—I could see them glancing and nodding at each other during the interview; a week later I was offered the position of business manager starting that summer. I was ecstatic—it was exactly the kind of job I had hoped to land. Mary too was thrilled about moving back to New York City, where she had first connected with Trungpa Rinpoche and where she still had many friends. The Boulder experience had been pretty much what we imagined—occasionally inspiring, socially frenetic and professionally frustrating. We did not feel the move would lessen our connection—we were likely to see as much if not more of our teachers as members of a smaller community that they visited frequently.

Mary and I bounced down the FDR Drive one scorching day in July 1983 to begin our new life in Brooklyn. I quickly began to appreciate the city's distinctive pace and jazz. My new job was hard but I had the support of the senior Quakers who had hired me and I kept abreast of the learning curve, steep though it was. My position felt right, because I felt a strong affinity with the Brooklyn meeting members in their determination to maintain a contemplative spirituality in the teeth of the speed of the city. Mary quickly found PR work with a big drug rehab program, and we moved into a spacious apartment in a friend's house in Park Slope. The New York Shambhala Center was a dynamic place that occupied a big loft on East 21st Street in Manhattan, and we were soon drawn into its activities. (Wendy, my earliest sangha friend in Boulder, had also moved to the city and had quickly found her feet. She had taken the leadership position of practice coordinator, a position that is often tough to fill. Buddhist practice, whether sitting meditation or the more elaborate tantric practices, is quite arduous and people get lazy about it. Not so Wendy, as dedicated a practitioner as I have ever met. Students like Wendy, who maintain their discipline across the years and decades, serve as an inspiration to the rest of us.) Basically, within weeks of landing in New York, Mary and I were convinced we'd been right— we belonged in an active city center far from the hub of Boulder. New York City was it.

There was one source of regret, however. The monthly arrival of Mary's period began to have a funereal quality as we tried and tried and failed to conceive. I had been tested before we left Boulder and had checked out okay. Mary kept charts and schedules and we began to attend a clinic in midtown Manhattan. Some of her hormone levels tested low and she began taking a mild fertility drug. Nothing worked. Her clock was ticking and as time passed it was tough to stay optimistic. I remember talking with Carolyn Gimian, Rinpoche's main editor, when she visited New York to teach—she was about Mary's age and she and her husband were having the same difficulty. We were both fatalistic about our prospects and could not see pursuing adoption.

The year after moving to New York was a dramatic one in my development as a dharma student. Shortly after settling in I flew back to Boulder to attend the *abhisheka* or empowerment of Vajrayogini, the tantric deity whose sadhana is traditionally the first liturgy practiced in Trungpa Rinpoche's lineage. This was The Big One for which I had spent hundreds of hours completing the ngöndro practices. I did not know whether I would understand the practice, or even whether this mattered; I did know I was motivated by a combination of ambition and devotion, as I believe most Western students are. The ambition was not particularly for enlightenment, although tantra is the quick path that offers the prospect of enlightenment in a single lifetime. I thought this was unlikely in my case—I felt and still feel slow-witted and over-stretched when it came to the tantric teachings. My ambition was far more for the social and institutional prestige that came with completing such difficult practices and joining the elite ranks of the *sadhakas*, the people who practiced this sadhana. And also, of course, I was motivated by my devotion to Trungpa Rinpoche, who trusted me sufficiently to admit me into this very special club.

The abhisheka was scheduled to begin at 5 p.m., but we all knew that wouldn't happen—Tibetan time is not like Western time. The couple of hundred of us were eventually told to get dinner and come back at eight. Then we sat around the corridors of the Boulder center for hours in our alphabetized ranks, visiting and chatting. The Boss (another of his affectionate titles) signed in at precisely midnight, his careful handwriting forming perfect zeroes. Because the preliminaries had to be completed by Rinpoche with students in attendance who had already received the abhisheka, we novices still had to wait for hours. When we finally filed into the shrine room for the actual transmission it was dawn, and both the sun and the moon were in the sky.

Trungpa Rinpoche had long since dispensed with the trappings of his religious authority. He wore business suits or Zen robes and taught in English from a chair. However, the solemnity of abhisheka required a different manifestation, and it took my breath away. Rinpoche was seated on a huge throne at the southern end of the shrine room wearing a magnificent brocade *chuba* or teaching robe and his red crested pandita hat. In front of him were arrayed the sacred implements and symbolic offerings of Vajrayogini's tantric practice. He chanted in Tibetan, a language I had hardly ever heard him use. Methodically, the *chöpön* or shrine servant brought him further implements from the main shrine—brass cruets, an ornate curved knife, bowls fashioned from skulls—that he flourished in front of us. The sight, together with our advanced fatigue, was sufficient to stop our collective mind. We sat there transfixed as the mysterious ceremony unfolded in front of us. On several occasions we filed in front of his throne to receive different blessings, including the conferring of a new name. Of course, there were also distinctive touches. At the precise moment of transmission, when the guru emanates the absolute, unstained nature of mind, Rinpoche was fast asleep, a glass of Guinness in front of him on his shrine table.

thirteen

Marty Janowitz is a great guy but he makes an unlikely soldier. This, however, is how he appeared to me one evening on a Greenwich Village sidewalk not long after my return from the Vajrayogini abhisheka in Boulder. Smart and affable, Marty was one of a group of Jewish guys who all attended Brandeis University and became Rinpoche's students in 1970, soon after his arrival in the US. He was from an Orthodox family in Queens, but here he was in New York City manifesting as a British field marshal, complete with dress uniform, Sam Brown belt and peaked cap. Marty had recently been chosen to succeed Perks as head of the kusung—his official title was kusung dapön, or commander of the kusung. I thought he looked droll; all he needed was a swagger stick to look like a stock character from a Sixties British film comedy. Marty, however, was in a thoughtful mood, as he sometimes is. He renewed his suggestion that I attend the next kasung encampment in Colorado, which he had first pitched to me at RMDC the previous year. At that time, I had muttered something about a difficult experience in the boy scouts and changed the subject. Now, as we waited for Rinpoche to arrive at a sangha member's apartment, I was more receptive. Marty explained that he himself had been mortified when offered promotion to such a senior military rank by Rinpoche. But look at me now, he said, gesturing to his uniform and laughing. I can "dapön it up" with the best of them.

I have always had the deepest respect for Janowitz and told him I would seriously consider his suggestion. This I must have begun to do because at the next major program we attended, the Kalapa Assembly of 1984, Mary and I elected to stay in the military wing of the hotel, in a whole separate building from the main program. With Janowitz's encouragement, I had begun to see my kusung role as where I "fit" in our organization, or *mandala,* as we preferred to call it. If this were the case, it made sense for me to embrace it more fully.

Kalapa Assembly was a similar program to Seminary, although of shorter duration and devoted exclusively to Rinpoche's presentation of the Shambhala teachings. By now, eight years after they had been introduced, these teachings were flourishing both within our community and as a graduated program for the general public known as Shambhala Training. The Shambhala tradition was an ancient one like buddhism, but it stressed a secular path rather than a religious or doctrinal one. Its exemplars were mythical rulers like Prince Ashoka of India, Gesar of Tibet, and Arthur and Charlemagne of the European tradition, and its ideal was the secular one of warriorship. Assembly was the event at which Rinpoche's role as a Shambhala ruler was fully manifest, at which students also received initiation to practice a special Shambhala sadhana he had composed.

The event was preceded by a transmission talk given by a senior student. In New York, the task fell to David Rome, another intellectual Jewish guy who for many years had been Rinpoche's private secretary. Rome was a fellow for whom, like Janowitz, I'd always had the highest regard, and I was relieved he would be presiding at the New York event, because the rumor was the transmission could be somewhat bizarre. I did not particularly feel this way in the aftermath, but I do recall David admonishing us to approach Assembly with "[our] imaginative rather than [our] critical faculties," advice that proved quite helpful.

We made the six-hour drive to Bedford Springs in western Pennsylvania with our entire wardrobe piled high in dry-cleaning bags on the back seat of our car. The Bedford Springs Hotel was a classic, white clapboard Victorian affair, large enough to accommodate three hundred of us. Rinpoche stayed in a suite on the top floor of a separate building that housed the kasung, in which Mary and I had an airy, comfortable room. Seminary had recently concluded at the same facility and a number of folks were staying on for the second program. There were plenty of old and new friends present, and we were enthusiastic about our participation. But the acclimation period proved somewhat brutal, because Rinpoche was in the process of inverting day and night and most of us were operating on a traditional schedule. The first talk began at two in the morning and we staggered off to bed around four. The second talk began even later—we got to bed around six, filled with misery and complaint. By the third night, however, the entire gathering (except the poor parents with infants) made the switch to the inverted schedule, which in turn, had a strange effect on ordinary events, which began to seem extraordinary. Breakfast would begin around five p.m., with lunch at around nine. Dinner was always a lengthy, formal affair that would begin around midnight and end at two or so. Then there was an hour or two of clean up and socializing before the main talk between four and five. We would all turn in between seven and eight and get up in the late afternoon to begin the next day's schedule.

Throughout Assembly, there was much emphasis on hierarchy, ritual and ceremony. Everyone had a distinct role at the program, and by extension, Shambhala society. Despite some lobbying and grumbling, most folks seemed to find a niche that suited them. In fact, social interaction felt remarkably harmonious and free from the kind of competitiveness that we were familiar with from Boulder. I had experienced some misgivings that Shambhala society might manifest somewhat like Fredonia in *Duck Soup*, with Rinpoche as Rufus T. Firefly. But to my delight, while humor was abundant, there was no frivolity or silliness. It was as if we were actually modeling what an enlightened society might feel like.

Maybe all this sounds preposterous. At Assembly I realized that there is indeed something preposterous at the core of Rinpoche's Shambhala vision, that you could infuse mundane reality with a sense of elegance and meaning by paying attention to detail and to each others' needs, by applying mindfulness and awareness to the business of daily living. Unlike Seminary where the schedule was tight and the discipline rigorous, the requirements at Assembly were more relaxed—people practiced a little, or not at all. There was much socializing and I had many wonderful encounters over meals and in people's rooms. Actually, the whole environment felt permeated and pacified by a sense of meditation, whether or not you were spending any time on the cushion. And whereas the sexual energy was again pretty high, at Kalapa Assembly I did not feel like a member of an endangered species as a married person as I might have at Seminary. In fact, the sense of stable partnership was at the core of Shambhala society, and I felt relieved and content to be there with my spouse.

Mary and I in fact saw little of each other during the day (or rather, the night). She was running the Regent's kitchen, and I spent a lot of time in Rinpoche's suite or involved in military activities. And each evening (early morning) the kusung division was responsible for serving dinner, a huge task. But we always came together before the talks, swapping stories of our day and visiting friends. And we steadily worked our way through our entire wardrobe, although I began to favor khakis for both day and evening wear; they constituted a more explicit military garb and therefore felt more comfortable.

Rinpoche did not so much teach at Assembly as simply manifest. At the evening (morning) event he might talk about Shambhala principles, or lead a group elocution lesson (being tutored in English pronunciation by a Tibetan felt particularly outrageous), or preside over a banquet or an awards ceremony. Whatever he was doing, he radiated great humor and warmth. Both Diana and the Regent were also there; Lady Diana, in particular, was in fine form. She gave one hilarious talk I attended in which she complained that "lack of foreplay was causing friction in the kingdom." The Regent seemed less at ease. His formal role in Shambhala society was somewhat vague, and he seemed to stay in the background during this event.

Throughout the program I would occasionally recall David Rome's invocation of my imaginative faculties. I found this to be my spontaneous response to the event, brought about largely by Rinpoche's skillful means rather than through any effort on my part. The inversion of day and night, the emphasis on ceremony and ritual, the attention to aesthetic detail and the principle of speech all worked together to create a heightened reality that extended over time and space, for the ten days or so we inhabited the Bedford Springs resort. And then, of course, Mary and I had to get into our car and drive back to our jobs in New York City. But organically there was an extension of this awareness upon return; you were able to see the magical qualities of ordinary life that had not been apparent before.

In the summer of that year I traveled again to Colorado to participate in the Magyal Pomra Encampment at Rocky Mountain Dharma Center. (Magyal Pomra is the lokapala or spiritual protector of RMDC. Tantric buddhism recognizes the existence of such guardian or protector spirits, similar to kami in the Japanese tradition.) Janowitz's blandishments and the inspiration of Kalapa Assembly propelled me there, despite my misgivings.

By its seventh year, encampment had blossomed from an ad hoc gathering of a few diehards into a major event that was open to all—no prior or further military commitment was required. With typical daring and creativity, Rinpoche had expanded kasung training from the purview of a small cadre of bodyguards into a whole separate stream of practice, education and instruction that reached hundreds of his students. The kasung now had its own texts, iconography, protocols and practices. And if RMDC was where Rinpoche always seemed to me to be in his element, the encampment grounds in the high meadow below Marpa Point were where he seemed in the element of his element.

But from the very start, the program was excruciating for me, and I hated it with waves of atavistic loathing. All the negative stereotypes from my scouting days flooded back. There was the same basic organization (platoons rather than patrols) and the same petty hierarchies of rank—*khenchen, kadö, rupön, dapon*—the array made my head spin. Then there was the same rigidity and disregard for common sense; the tiny pup tents in which we all slept were pitched not in relation to the contours of the land, but in military rows that cut straight across the steep hillsides. My own tent had a cavernous drop in the middle, for which my platoon leader gave me a scrap of plywood to try and level it out. Then there were the same regimented roll calls, the same inspections, the same salutes, the same moronic songs sung in front of flagpoles. I think by the first evening I was already fantasizing about escape, about feigning some dreadful illness and being stretchered off the mountain. But something told me this was shameful and cowardly and I should try and stick it out.

Did I mention the pup tents in which we slept? At encampment I did not sleep. I writhed in misery, trying to find a comfortable position on the uneven, rocky ground. At eight thousand feet, nights were cold even in August and I shivered in my thin sleeping bag. I took big belts from a jug of bourbon I had brought, hoping to knock myself out. If I did finally drop off around dawn, sleeping late was impossible because by eight the interior of the tent became an inferno. I stewed in silent resentment, but there was no one to whom I could really confide my misery. My best friend Wendy was there as a cook, but she was accompanied by the guy who would become her first husband, and I did not see much of her. Some friends from New York were also there, but I did not know them well yet. Janowitz was there, of course, but I put on a brave face for his benefit, telling him I was having a fine old time. But after three days without sleep I wondered how I would possibly keep going through the event.

In marked contrast to my own beleaguered state, Rinpoche presided over the proceedings with what was clearly huge satisfaction. He had inaugurated the event with a giant *lhasang* (a ceremonial offering of juniper smoke) at a fire pit at the bottom of the parade ground. Then he retired to his tent at the top of the meadow, a splendid white pavilion embroidered with Tibetan snow lions. There he typically spent each day sitting out front under a canopy, watching the day's activities unfold from a canvas director's chair. There were always people visiting him, coming and going. And there was plenty to watch, because as always at our programs, there was a succession of carefully planned activities. The basic kasung practice was drill, in which careening phalanxes of novices like me (the veterans called us "turtles") would practice marching around the parade ground. There was *kyudo* practice, or Zen archery, led by Shibata Sensei, the imperial bow maker to the Japanese court who had begun teaching in our community at Rinpoche's invitation. The equestrians were there, with their splendid horses and traveling stable. There was a big shrine tent in which there were talks, meditation (with boots on), even a wedding. And there was all the daily hubbub of activity entailed in running such a big event outdoors. I was in significant despair that I seemed unable to appreciate any of this.

It was not all unrelieved misery. Each evening after nightfall we would gather around campfires and behave like I imagine soldiers everywhere do—we would drink, smoke and tell dirty stories. There was much hilarity and camaraderie. At one of these gatherings, I offered a rendition of the famous English hymn of Blake's *Jerusalem*, which had been one of our school songs back in Yorkshire. An Englishwoman on the opposite side of the campground heard me and made it across to our fire site by the second verse, which we belted out together. We then proceeded to see off most of the bourbon I had brought as we swapped stories from our childhood. I did get some sleep that night because I passed out fully clothed as soon as I crawled into my tent.

I awoke quite late next morning remembering that I was scheduled for a kusung shift with Rinpoche. I staggered over to his tent with a blinding hangover to find the overnight kusung very pissed off by my tardiness. She (by this time, both male and female kusung served Rinpoche) told me to go in and announce myself—Rinpoche had just woken and was ready to get up and get dressed.

I tiptoed into the curtained area of the pavilion where Rinpoche slept in a bed on a leveled plywood platform. The kusung was clearly mistaken because he was still fast asleep. I advanced cautiously to the side of the bed when Rinpoche suddenly wheeled upright and yelled "PHAT!" in my face. This had become a favorite trick of his, to jolt us out of wandering mind with sudden ambushes. Perks had commissioned an antique cannon for him in Vermont, which now sat at the bottom of the parade ground. Rinpoche would have it fired every morning at flag break, but also on other, unannounced occasions, which would wake every single person on the RMDC property out of whatever daydream he or she was engaged in at that moment. Then everyone would laugh, because the joke was always on us, and we loved him, that he would play it on us. I'm sure in my normal state I would have leapt several feet in the air at Rinpoche's bedside trick, but I was so hung over that my mind was like sludge, and I merely smiled.

Good morning, sir, I managed. Did you sleep well?

Very well, he said, stretching.

I went to get the tea for the shrines and for his breakfast. When I returned to help him get dressed I considered telling him that I was having a lousy time, but he would ask me why and I would be obliged to confess that I felt stuck around my issues with hierarchy and regimentation. It seemed so small-minded I couldn't bring myself to mention it. So I said nothing as I struggled get the belly strap of his military pants fastened. Rinpoche packed some weight, and the pants, made of heavy cavalry twill, seemed just too small. When I finally got the button fastened and zipped up the fly, I said to him,

The pants seem a bit tight, sir.

No, Rinpoche demurred. They're just right.

Then he told me that the belly strap fastened across the *hara,* the Japanese term for the spot three fingers below the navel that is the source of *chi,* or the life force. Clothing should always remind you of your chi, Rinpoche explained to me. It was another lesson I would re-member. Rinpoche had guessed that it was me singing the Victorian hymn the night before and asked me to repeat it for him. He seemed intrigued by Blake's conflation of spiritual and martial imagery, and we talked about what Blake might mean by "Satanic mills." Rinpoche had no bias whatsoever toward other traditions of wisdom and was clearly fascinated by Blake's poetry.

The next twenty-four hours marked my low point. That evening a number of dignitaries arrived, including the Regent, David Rome, and Dr. Mitchell Levy, who was both Diana Mukpo's lover and Rinpoche's personal physician. I sought out Mitchell and asked him whether he had any sleeping pills he could let me have. (I think I imagined that doctors traveled with a black bag containing a stethoscope, a rubber mallet and all kinds of basic medicines.) It was a measure of my desperation that I would approach someone I barely knew with such a request. Mitchell apologized—doctors in general did not have problems with insomnia, he said. He mentioned that the Regent might have sleeping pills, but wasn't sure he would part with them. I ended my quest there and returned to my tent, where I faced another night of sleeplessness and misery.

The next morning at flag break I had had enough. As we all sang one of Rinpoche's guard songs, I started to choke with frustration and despair. Here I am, stuck in the middle of this guy's stupid trip, I told myself angrily. I can't keep doing this. But simultaneously I recognized that my extraordinary teacher had only one trip, which was the libera-tion of all beings from suffering, and if I had a problem it was because I was too petty and arrogant to appreciate his vision. I started to choke up and "fell out" from my formation, seeking a stand of aspen outside the camp perimeter where I could be alone. There I fell apart, shaking and heaving with great gulping sobs of shame. No one saw me and I was able to eventually gather myself and feel a little better. I realized that all my negativity and resistance had come to a head and, like pus from a boil, something poisonous felt like it been expelled. I returned to my platoon and our day's activities. And on some basic level, from that point on, I gave up.

The first difference I noticed was that I began to enjoy drill. Drill is a kind of meditation in action, but instead of keeping your attention on your breath, you keep it on your stride, your drill sergeant's instructions and the guy next to you. Unless you do this carefully, you screw up, miss a step, miss a turn or stumble in general. Until this point I had found drill pointless and difficult. I particularly objected to the dumb chants we would shout out to keep marching rhythm. Now I found that if I silenced my carping mind, drill was actually fun. Even the calls and response began to strike me as okay.

Encampment exposed my core problem with exceptionalism, which goes something like this. I may pay lip service to the notion of humility, but secretly I believe I'm hot shit. I continue to turn up at talks given by Trungpa Rinpoche and wait for him to scan the crowd, notice me (like he did at the very first seminar), crook a finger and beckon me to sit in the middle of the front row, my rightful place. If this doesn't happen today, then it will eventually, because surely he will recognize how exceptional I am (despite some minor flaws).

And Trungpa Rinpoche did have the amazing capacity to make every single one of us feel special, that he had absolutely no problem with who we were, that he in fact loved us not despite who we were, but because of who we were. At the same time he also stressed that each one of us was zilch, a grain of sand, a root vegetable that needed to be boiled in the stewpot so long that we had no color, no individuality, no claim to fame. This denial of exceptionalism is the other side of the same coin, but is obviously much less appealing to us (at least, it was to me). In meditation, you continuously experience nothingness, the emptiness of mind, but your personal movie always roars back in Technicolor, the star of which is always the same person—the brilliant, exceptional YOU. In drill practice, you really did become nothing, a mere part of a whole, and it was counterproductive to stand out—it made you mess up. For the duration of the practice, however long, you could literally disappear. It also helped if your posture was good, if you marched with your head and shoulders erect, because you could hear and respond more effectively. Egolessness and dignity—these were the essence of what Rinpoche was trying to teach us at encampment.

In conventional terms, it makes no sense at all that a buddhist teacher would utilize military forms to teach nonaggression, which is the heart of the buddhist path. In fact, it's counterintuitive, because the military model institutionalizes and legitimizes the practice of violence in our society. But Trungpa Rinpoche was not a conventional teacher. He utilized the rituals of military culture to channel our unruly energy in a uniquely uplifting way. With its uniformity and communal culture, encampment had the flavor of a peculiarly vivid monasticism, as if our caps and uniforms represented a uniquely Western version of shaved scalps and robes. It conferred a tremendous feeling of freedom and dignity. Other parties were obviously less than convinced of our benign intent. At intervals during the week, a helicopter would sweep low over the encampment ground, a dark clad figure leaning from a doorway, filming with a powerful video camera. We assumed it was the FBI, keeping tabs on out activities. We must have seemed to them like a gang of paramilitary whackos. At first we waved, then learned to ignore the intrusion.

If I had any remaining doubts about my extraordinary good fortune to be at this program, they were dispelled later that day. As I went about my business I noticed that Rinpoche had a new visitor, a small, copper-skinned fellow wearing a long gray braid and an old suit, who was sitting next to him under the canopy of his pavilion. I asked different folks who he might be but no one seemed to know. As the afternoon wore on, I noticed that the visitor had left, that Rinpoche was now sitting alone. Then something weird began to happen. The Colorado Rockies have a dry summer climate, with occasional violent thunderstorms. The high cumulus clouds suddenly began to darken and loom lower. The wind whipped up. Then quickly, the sky turned very dark, almost black. Then the rain began. This was not rain like I had ever experienced before. It descended in steel rods that leveled our tents, generated rivers through the campsite, and sent us huddling for shelter beneath the few large canopies that were left standing. We tried to express our amazement, but couldn't hear each other speak over the roar of the storm. I tried to look across at Rinpoche's tent, but visibility was nil. We laughed and hooted. Then just as suddenly as the rain had begun, it ended, and the sun came out. As we stumbled out to inspect the damage and begin to clean up, something really remarkable happened. A dazzling rainbow appeared in the middle of the campsite, spanning the hundred feet between the lhasang hearth and the front of Rinpoche's tent. At its apex it was only fifteen feet high—I had never seen anything so vivid or extraordinary. Everyone gaped and suddenly the identity of the mysterious visitor circulated around the camp. He was Gerald Red Elk, a Sioux medicine man who had come to pay his respects to the Tibetan "chief." Later, the exchange before Red Elk's departure was also circulated around the camp.

Rinpoche: I think it will rain tomorrow morning.

Red Elk: I think it will rain soon.

Rinpoche: Ah yes. You're right.

There was no other explanation that fit the circumstances other than that these two shamans engaged in a friendly contest of conjuring the elements. The suddenness and severity of the storm was something otherworldly, and the rainbow that sealed its disappearance could not have been an accidental phenomenon. It was a supernormal event, of the kind that Tibetan scripture speaks often, that Trungpa Rinpoche always firmly abjured when asked to demonstrate. The temptation of Red Elk's challenge must have proved irresistible.

However, my mental grumbling did not come to a full stop after my meltdown in the woods. There was still Skirmish to negotiate, an all-day event that was held on a huge stretch of national forest land further into the mountains behind Marpa Point. The point of exercise was never fully clear to me, but it was clearly A Big Deal. The entire camp was divided into two teams that were pitted against each other like opposing sides in a giant chess match. Rinpoche sat on the hillside to observe the strategy of the two "armies." There were weapons in the form of flour bombs, platoons of scouts, commandos, engineers, saboteurs, you name it. (The first-ever Skirmish was a famous fiasco in which the two armies, led by David Rome and the Regent, indulged in an orgy of flour-bomb carnage and were then required by Rinpoche to repeat the exercise, having been admonished for completely missing the point.) I was content to be a lowly scout and be told where to hide and what to do.

My comrades and I were to conceal ourselves and ambush any marauders from the opposing army and capture them. We saw no one all day, sitting behind an outcrop of rock in a dream-like state in which desultory chatter was interspersed by long periods of total silence. Like the clouds overhead, my complaints and objections would scud across my mind, vanish and reform themselves, without lasting substance or permanence. Then late in the afternoon a siren sounded, and the war game was over. I never found out who won, nor did I care.

The next day was the last full day of the program, and I realized the distance I had traveled. Perhaps it was just relief that it was over, but great waves of joy began to wash over me. The immediate precipitant was the visit of the "civilians," regular folk who were attending other programs at RMDC's main facility. They seemed so sloppily dressed and confused compared with the khaki-clad, purposeful members of encampment. They also seemed amorphous, almost generic—civilians, after all. By contrast, the individuality of the kasung was brilliantly on display, as if by becoming no one, people became themselves. Civilian friends stayed for dinner and for the evening campfire; I tried to explain what I had been through, but found it impossible. I slept soundly that night, and next day I became quite emotional on taking my leave of all the people I'd met, which surprised me. More surprises were in store, however, when I descended to the main buildings with my gear.

I had been at encampment for only a week, but it was clear I was not the same person who had made the trip up the mountain. I was simply aglow with a calm, radiant happiness. I also seemed to be able to anticipate what people were thinking and what they were about to say. No matter how petty or selfish their concerns, I could and did sympathize with their difficulties. My elation sustained me all the way to the Denver airport, from where I called home (after some difficulty remembering my phone number). The food at the airport cafeteria was the most delicious I had ever tasted. I bought a copy of *The New York Times* to read on the plane, in which the complex global problems described seemed completely soluble from my new aerial perspective. I believe I was in that state described in buddhist scripture as *mahasukha*, the great joy that comes from the experience of egolessness. The psychiatric community has a different term for the state, which I would learn in due course.

fourteen

My elevated mood continued after I returned to New York. I was bursting with energy, and quickly discovered my inner sexual primate. After helping me bathe for the first time in ten days, my wife discovered me swinging from the rafters in the bedroom, yodeling like Tarzan. She was a good sport about this development, which lasted a full week. I began sleeping like a lamb, returning to school with renewed vigor. Nothing in my daily life felt like an obstacle, and I relished the challenge of work. And I still felt an active connection to the vivid military world I had just left. Uncannily, although I had resumed my business garb of coat and tie, I could still feel the clasp of the web belt grabbing my waist and the military cap catching my forehead as I went about my day. I had returned from encampment in an altered state.

And then Rinpoche arrived. Our brownstone in Brooklyn had become the "visit house," and about a week after encampment ended Rinpoche and party arrived en route to retreat in Nova Scotia. When he entered our house it took some restraint on my part not to break protocol and hug him—I was so grateful for my encampment experience that I wanted to tell him about it and thank him personally. Helping him down the stairs on his first morning, I did manage to tell him I'd taken to heart his advice about clothing as a reminder of chi—I said I could feel my military uniform all the time, even though I was no longer wearing it. So can I, he said, smiling. I got him settled into his armchair and he did something odd. He took a packet of Rothman's cigarettes and a gold lighter from his suit pocket and placed them on the side table. I had not set out an ashtray and went to find one. In the ten days of encampment, I had not seen Rinpoche smoke once.

Rinpoche, I didn't know you still smoked, I said on my return.

I forget, he said with a shrug.

It struck me as somehow typical that Rinpoche would need to remind himself to indulge a habit that for most smokers is very tough to break. Smoking for him was an intentional act that he nevertheless had to remind himself to do. The other thing that struck me about Rinpoche on this visit was that he'd become somewhat frail. Despite his handicap, Rinpoche was always robust and strong. In Brooklyn he seemed to have a new difficulty getting up from a seated or lying position. It is likely his slow physical decline began around this time. Certainly, during the retreat he took that fall at Mill Village, Nova Scotia, he became more and more detached from the concrete, physical world. He taught seminaries and led programs in both 1985 and 1986, but began to communicate increasingly sparingly until his death in April 1987.

My assistant at Brooklyn Friends School was a gracious woman who owned an apartment in Brooklyn and a spacious home in the Hamptons on Long Island, where wealthy New Yorkers have their summer places. That fall she invited us to spend a weekend with them; a rich friend was throwing a lavish birthday party at his beachfront home, complete with fireworks display. She also told me confidentially that she had a "lucky" guest room—her nephew and his wife had recently conceived their first child there. So Mary and I drove out there happily, curious to visit this famous playground of the rich. I felt a little odd parking our battered Toyota alongside the Rolls Royces and Mercedes on the beachfront, and I became inexplicably sad lying in the sand, watching the profligacy of thirty thousand dollars worth of fireworks explode in the sky. That night I could not fall asleep in the lucky guest room. To borrow a phrase from Salman Rushdie, the Hamptons stay was the first crow in the sky, a speck of darkness that would later become a flock, then a barrage, and eventually an avalanche.

My second year as business manager of the Friends' school turned out to be rough. I had been hired in part as support for the principal, a beleaguered woman in her first head's job who was battling some ornery veteran teachers for control of the school. We had a strong alliance during the first year, and I had advised her through some unpopular decisions. We got along well, and I was an occasional guest at her weekend home outside the city. At the start of the second year the school hired two new staffers who had distinct attributes I did not share—they were both women and also senior Quakers. Now the head had allies who were truly her peers and her door was increasingly closed to me. Our relationship became awkward and chilly and I felt my gender to be increasingly a problem. My main ally among the trustees, a Quaker businessman who had adopted me as his protégé, was taking a year's sabbatical and so I felt newly isolated in my responsibilities. And then there was my insomnia. Starting with the visit to Long Island I had seemingly lost my ability to fall asleep naturally and visited a doctor for a check-up. He pronounced me in perfect health and cautioned me that the typical cause of insomnia was depression. I told him I didn't feel depressed and he gave me sleeping pills. I soldiered on, thinking the problem would lift, but also painfully aware that my high spirits of just a month earlier had evaporated.

As fall became winter my mood darkened, and unmedicated sleep became impossible. I finally confronted the principal and told her I felt I'd lost her trust and that my morale and job performance were suffering as a result. She seemed genuinely surprised and was clearly unaware of the extent to which her battle formation had been realigned to my cost. She offered me more regular meetings, but it was a futile gesture, because basically I'd switched from the ranks of her allies to those with grievances against her. My tenure at the school was likely doomed from this moment forth. And then came the trip to England.

At Christmas we set off to visit my kin, including my parents, despite my sister's warning that my mother, who had been hospitalized and re-released during the previous year, was not in good shape. This turned out to be an understatement. My mother was in fact in a state of catatonia, unable even to watch television, never mind prepare meals or hold a conversation. A pall of morbidity hung over my parents' neglected household, my distraught father insisting he could not go on living with her in this state. I began to sense a pattern in her illness, one characterized by adverse reaction to the dereliction on the part of the men in her life. Her father had neglected and abused her, her husband had kicked her out and her only son had, of course, abandoned her to live abroad. Thus I was a cause of her suffering. Stricken with guilt, I walked out to a pay phone in the village to call my sister. Her answer machine picked up, and I remembered that she was away visiting her in-laws. I felt an awful despair.

By the time we got back to London I was a wreck. We discussed what I should do on my return and agreed that I would consult with some of the senior folk at the New York Shambhala Center. It never crossed my mind to see a mental-health professional, a typical sangha prejudice at the time. A friend came to visit and I shocked him by weeping in the taxi on the way to the airport. I honestly did not know what was happening to me, or what would happen next.

Well, I went back to work, after a fashion. I developed some robotic ability to continue functioning, but I was beginning to lose track of details and make mistakes. My assistant observed these developments with growing alarm, and suggested I talk to the principal about taking time off. In February I did this and stayed home for a few days, but my absence only made my feelings of guilt more acute. I went back to work in a state of complete bewilderment and found I could not even remember how to operate the copy machine, or decipher columns of numbers on a page. My assistant found me trembling and weeping at my desk. She told me to go home and take a proper leave; she would cover for me. I did so, writing a letter to the trustees requesting a one-month leave of absence. Then I picked up the phone and called the Vajra Regent Ösel Tendzin.

The Regent had taken several such calls in my presence, and I think we were both aware of the irony that it was now my turn to plead for his support and advice. Predictably, he was very understanding and helpful, and responded to the gravity of my mental state without either minimizing it or buying into my sense of personal drama. I was bolstered by our conversation, if only because a person I trusted so profoundly was now aware of my predicament. Tellingly, it never crossed my mind to call Trungpa Rinpoche. I would have been too embarrassed, too ashamed to confess my pitiful state to him. The Regent was an Italian-American from New Jersey; Rinpoche was a Tibetan from some cosmic realm that awed and inspired me. Had I seen Rinpoche in person I would likely have buckled and asked for his advice—you were always completely transparent in his presence anyway. But I could not have picked up a phone and called him. I could not do that. But it was not simply shame that prevented my calling him. Diana Mukpo, in her memoir, recounts how Rinpoche was cheerfully chatting on the phone with an old friend the day after their wedding, telling his friend of this amazing development in his life. He had to cup the mouthpiece with his hand and ask Diana to remind him of her name. He'd forgotten it! I'd also relayed calls to him from students with whom he was much closer than me, and he would repeatedly pantomime, Who is it? Who is it? during the call. I could not take the risk that Rinpoche would similarly blank on my identity—there were several other English guys in the sangha with whom he could have confused me, as Allen Ginsberg often did.

It is difficult to find words to describe how I felt over the ensuing weeks. People may imagine that buddhism, as a nontheistic religion, does not predicate the existence of either a heaven or a hell. Well, it certainly does, along with several other psychological states that humans may experience; however it defines such states as ultimately temporary because they are contingent on ego. Mental illness is one human experience of hell. The terror and bewilderment I felt were similar to my experience after Belfast, only much more intense—I had waves of panic attacks for the first time. The scalding sense of shame and failure was also more acute; I felt vividly repugnant to myself. Again, the loss of basic functions like concentration, short-term memory and the ability to eat was terrifying. And behind it all the indignation—how could this be happening to *me?* Catastrophe was what happened to *others!* The kid in elementary school who'd had polio and wore a leg caliper; the kid who tripped in the street and got hit by a car and disfigured—these things didn't happen to *me!* When I finally dragged David Rome out to Brooklyn weeks later to see me, he was very firm about this naïveté. No, he said, his voice rising in our friend's living room, where I sat stricken and shaking. It happens to *you!* It happens to *you!* He was also very quick to discredit my specious logic about suicide, which was very helpful for me to hear.

Suicide, of course, is the major threat for people who become as depressed as I was. Fleeting and involuntary at first, the siren-call of oblivion becomes steadily more insistent until it becomes a clamorous obsession. Like others whose accounts I have read—Styron, Roth, Ginsberg—I became fixated on literary heroes who had taken their own lives, whose examples seemed to give the act a spurious, morbid glamour. What restrained me was not mere physical cowardice (although this did play a role), but the awareness that my death by my own hand would effectively destroy my mother's life (I felt my wife might be better off without me) and also the knowledge, lucidly explained in the early books of Chögyam Trungpa, that suicide by beings in the hell realm is futile and only intensifies their suffering. In fact, there were two major sources of comfort for me during the excruciating month I spent in our Brooklyn apartment before I sought real professional help—the music of the Beatles and the writings of Chögyam Trungpa. No matter how savagely I judged myself, he did not do so. In particular, his chapter on "Disappointment" in *The Myth of Freedom* became an important text for me.

My disappointment was indeed of epic proportions. Ironically, my arrival in New York had not only fulfilled my professional ambitions. Since seminary I had been steadily occupying positions of greater visibility in the sangha, and during my second winter in New York I was invited to become the resident co-director of Shambhala Training in the city, a position of significant prestige. I accepted the appointment, even though by this time I was feeling very shaky. Eve, my co-director, was a good friend whom I was able to take into my confidence and spend time with during my leave. She was concerned about me, but hopeful I could step up to my role before long. I was not so sanguine, feeling it was unacceptable that such a pitiful specimen as I should present himself as any kind of representative of warriorship. Indeed, during this period, I found myself avoiding the premises of the Shambhala Center loft, lest I be tempted to cast myself to oblivion from its 11th story windows. Some warrior! Eventually, Eve released me from the pretense of my role, and someone else took the position.

Shocking as it now seems to me, I was determined to undergo this experience of depression without recourse to medication. I still took a hypnotic to sleep, but disdained anything I deemed "anesthesia," a refusal based on both ignorance and pride. I still believed antidepressant medication was a poison that had driven my mother mad, but more importantly, I felt I belonged to an elite community that understood the illusory nature of ego, which the psychiatric profession of course did not. Psychiatrists were therefore to be distrusted, even disdained. I did consult with a number of specialists in the treatment of insomnia (as if this was a cause, not a symptom of my disorder) and also began seeing a psychologist who happened to specialize in drug addiction. In hindsight, this interaction was actively harmful, because talk therapy, unless very narrowly focused, is useless with severely depressed individuals since they have lost all perspective. Thus excavating my childhood and adolescence served only to confirm my sense of worthlessness. And his insistence that I was experiencing infantile regression only made me more stricken with shame and hopelessness.

Amazingly, despite already having suffered one episode and having understood my mother's illness, I had not named my illness as clinical depression. I still felt I was suffering from an anxiety disorder provoked by feelings of guilt and my problems at work. I tried "holistic" cures—I took massage, acupuncture, swam at the YMCA. I spent time with friends in the New York sangha, many of whom were very kind. But my mood continued to worsen and my anxiety to escalate. Matters came to a head one evening when I felt could no longer tolerate my mental anguish and went to the local Emergency Room. After waiting several hours I eventually consulted with a young intern who took my blood pressure and asked me in a thick Brooklyn accent about suicidal intent. I said I had continuous ideation (I knew the vocabulary by now) but had no intention of acting upon it. He told me I was just feeling "pent up," and whatever made me feel less pent up, I should "just go do dat." He was not able to prescribe anything, but suggested instead I go home and make an appointment to see a psychiatrist. This became something of a private joke after I began to recover—feeling "pent up" becoming a codeword for the most ludicrous of euphemisms.

I did, however, take the young doctor's advice and see a psychiatrist, who was a member of the sangha. After a handful of questions, he was able to diagnose my condition instantly. Tellingly, he diagnosed me as unipolar, and did not characterize my recent elevation of mood as hypomania; he saw it rather as genuine spiritual experience (I've since concluded it was both). He prescribed a sedative and an antidepressant that

I began taking hungrily—all resistance to mainstream treatment was now spent. To my amazement and relief, despite some unpleasant side effects, I began to feel noticeably better within days. My leave from the school was about to expire and instead of resigning I shocked everyone by turning up back at work. I tried to pick up the reins again, firing on about half my cylinders. But understandably my long absence had fatally spooked the trustees, and they had already decided to replace me. Because they could not fire me for being ill, they reviewed the books and found enough errors to fire me for incompetence, about a week after my return. It was an irrevocable blow, the abrupt end of my magical ascension to the profession I had coveted. With nothing now to do, and with a modest buyout of my contract in the bank, we decided to leave the city.

fifteen

The untold story in narratives of major depression is often the appalling toll on the immediate family of the sick person. Although my wife only quit her job when I was finally fired from mine, her full-time task for many months had basically been getting me through the day. She came with me to almost all my appointments, often sitting through the whole interview. She read and researched constantly and called people for advice. And she checked on me by phone every day when I was marooned in our apartment, pacing and smoking. Basically her own needs were subsumed by mine for the best part of a year. Tellingly, after I recovered and she decided to enroll in graduate school, she chose clinical social work, specializing in psychiatric disorders. I guess she figured she had a calling.

Fortunately Mary had been feeling fed up with her job anyway and we had a quiet, convenient place to go, so our move out of the city suited both of us. Her family owned a farmhouse in Vermont that was little used in the spring months, and we moved up there in mid-April. My New York psychiatrist had pronounced my job loss to be a "red herring," meaning that it was logical to feel depressed after such an event, and I should not expect any rapid recovery. He was right, and for a time I began to feel sharply worse. The injustice of my firing from the school stung me deeply, and I became mired in self-pity. The thought of working in another school, of working anywhere, seemed impossibly far-fetched. But the Vermont property was comfortable and peaceful, and we settled into routines of walking and reading that were agreeable. I was actually able to read *Middlemarch*, which meant my powers of concentration were returning; I was also eating slightly better. But my overall mood felt stuck, despite the big doses of medication I was taking.

After three weeks we headed back to New York so I could check in with my psychiatrist. I recall him gloomily scanning the questionnaire I completed in his office, on which I'd clearly checked all the wrong boxes. He said he didn't think medication alone was doing me much good and I should try psychotherapy again, which was the last thing I wanted to hear.

Then we learned that the Regent was about to visit Boston. I hadn't spoken with him since my panicked call in February and was eager to see him in person if I could. We drove up to Boston Shambhala Center, which in that era was housed in a former Orthodox church in Newton. Presenting myself to the Regent in the state I was in felt akin to putting my head into the lion's mouth, because I felt a distinct risk that he might challenge me in some difficult way, which I could not have handled. He spied me hovering nearby during the reception after his talk and eventually made his way over to me, regarding me sideways, his head tilted backwards.

You crazy, Cape? he asked.

No, sir.

Just sad?

Yes, sir.

Don't do anything stupid.

No, sir, I managed, realizing Rome must have told him of my preoccupation with suicide. Then he leant forward more intimately.

You just need to do nothing for a while. And allow yourself to be disappointed. Can you do that?

Yes, sir.

Allow yourself to be disappointed, he repeated.

Then someone else caught his attention, and he turned away.

I date my recovery from that moment. He was so kind, so accepting, and his words were such balm to my soul that I may have become tearful. When we returned to New York I felt a new resolve. We sat down, looked at the numbers and decided to pull up stakes for the summer and move back to Karmê Chöling, the meditation center in Vermont where we had met six years earlier. Jenny, the director, listened to my story with calm sympathy and then invited me to take part in the center's activities to whatever degree I wished. This suited me just fine and I quickly chose a combination of a little meditation and a lot of running the wood splitter, an ancient contraption that processed firewood for the wood furnace in the main house. The simple outdoor work was a tonic for me, as was the fact that my partner on the wood crew was the redoubtable Peter Orlovsky, who happened to be in worse psychological shape than I was, which was saying something.

Orlovsky was well known to me from Boulder and New York as Allen Ginsberg's partner. He and Allen were stalwart members of the New York center, where Peter could be relied upon to supply the lustiest voice in chanting. He was tall and handsome with a thick, gray ponytail, and he was much loved. But most of the members of his large family suffered from mental illness, and by the mid-80s Peter had developed some severe problems of his own. When I met up with him at Karmê Chöling he had been recently released from New York's Bellevue Hospital where he'd been confined after threatening a girlfriend with a machete and a subsequent police siege of his apartment in the East Village. He was also struggling to stay clean and sober and seemed pretty shaky. We didn't talk much as we ran the splitter, but took pride in working quickly and amassing mountains of cordwood. However, Peter's energy gradually escalated into mania and after an all-night session of compulsive floor mopping, he had to return to the city where I heard he was hospitalized again.

There were plenty of ghosts on the Karmê Chöling property. Mary resumed her old job in the front office, but I stuck with maintenance and kitchen work rather than tackle PR again, and in that capacity, I became aware that a number of the longer-staying residents were recovering from depressive illness as I was; we formed a kind of secret society. One woman confided in me that she had bipolar disorder and was recovering from a recent severe episode.

You been in the bin? she asked. I been in the bin.

No, I told her.

I wouldn't trade it, though, she said.

I asked her what she meant. She meant that she would not trade the manic high she had experienced for respite from the depression that followed. I realized that I probably would not have either and that this was both very foolish and very selfish of me.

Gradually, as I began to feel useful, my sense of humor began to return. We moved around from room to room for a while, until an old cabin near the main house became vacant and we moved in there. I decided I had received all the help I was going to get from medication and flushed my antidepressants down the toilet. And then I was asked to do something that I knew how to do, that I could do well and that made all the difference. Jenny asked me whether I would take charge of service for that summer's visiting teacher, Jamgön Kongtrul Rinpoche. I hesitated, and told her my confidence level still felt pretty low. Airily, Jenny said she was sure I'd be fine. No one on the staff had my level of experience of kusung service, she explained, and she needed someone to train other people in the house. I was the logical choice. What did I say?

Well, I said shakily. I'll have to go back to New York to get my suits.

No problem, she said pleasantly.

I eventually drove down to the city in July to a hot apartment full of dead flies. The next day I drove back up with my dress suits and Wendy, who was on her way to Karmê Chöling to do a cabin retreat. As we drove past Yankee Stadium listening to the Live Aid concert by satellite from London, life didn't seem so bad after all. Wendy reliably makes me feel grateful to be alive, and I sensed that the worst was behind me. And there was the visit of Jamgön Rinpoche to look forward to, a man who fit the definition of a prince more fully than anyone I had ever met.

When His Holiness the Sixteenth Karmapa left Tibet for exile in India in 1959, he brought with him four young boys who were all tulkus, or incarnations of senior Kagyu lamas. Jamgön Kongtrul Rinpoche was the third incarnation of the great nineteenth-century teacher Lodrö Thaye, whose accomplishments were so vast he is often referred to as the Tibetan Leonardo. After the Karmapa's death in 1981, the four tulkus became his regents until his new incarnation was found and trained (at the time of writing, the Seventeenth Karmapa is in his early twenties and lives in Dharamsala, India). For simplicity's sake we referred to these four young lamas as the Kagyu princes, and in the early '80s three of them (Jamgön, Situ and Shamar Rinpoches) visited our community in North America on separate occasions. Each was in his late twenties, spoke excellent English and was a wonderful teacher in his own right. Many of us made the strongest connection with Jamgön

Rinpoche, who seemed awed by Trungpa Rinpoche's achievements in the West and was eager to engage his students in a very personal and direct way. Unlike Trungpa Rinpoche, who had been born in a nomad's tent, Jamgön Rinpoche was from a wealthy, aristocratic family, so he literally had princely origins. But he was also a prince in the ulterior sense, in that he was unfailingly kind, wise and humble. He also had an impish sense of humor and seemed to genuinely appreciate his interactions with Western students. He was scheduled to stay at Karmê Chöling for several weeks, giving teachings and empowerments, along with two attending monks and a translator.

Jamgön Rinpoche's visit was the highlight of that summer. We installed him in the shrine room at the top of one of the new wings, a light airy space that we decorated with satin and brocade. In addition to his teaching schedule, he also held formal and informal interviews with residents of the house, many visitors and even a television crew from Burlington. He spoke beautiful English, but because the Karmapa had told him not to teach in English until he spoke it perfectly, his modesty always made him use an interpreter in formal teaching situations (although he would often correct what he thought was faulty translation). Because of my role, I was inseparable from him during his visit, and I grew to love him almost as much as I loved Trungpa Rinpoche. However, I was still struggling with a deep sense of humiliation about my recent experience, and after one public talk asked him a question about whether he felt Western students could really ever understand and practice tantra. When I held my ritual implements, I told him, I felt like a child brandishing a toy rattle and drum. He did not wait for a translation but answered animatedly in Tibetan. The interpreter said Rinpoche's view was that we fully deserved our teacher's trust in us. Many people were making great progress on the path of dharma, in his opinion. Yeah right, I thought to myself. Not me.

After the talk I rushed up to his suite to arrange for the tea service that he liked to enjoy fairly continuously. From his armchair where he sat chatting with people seated on the floor, he spied me in the doorway and beckoned me to enter. I awkwardly began removing my shoes but he gestured that that was unnecessary—he wanted to speak to me right away. I advanced and crouched by his chair. I don't recall his words, just the gentle insistence of his voice and the compassion in his beautiful round face. He basically told me I was a worthy student and had nothing to apologize for, as if he understood perfectly what had motivated my question. I feel very fortunate that I ever met such a remarkable being.

As the summer wound down, I decided to take a two-week cabin retreat; I felt well enough to be alone with my mind and my meditation cushion. Before my retreat ended another senior lama, Thrangu Rinpoche, would arrive and I could expect to be involved in more service with him. However, a week or so into the retreat, which I shared happily with a swarm of mice, a visitor showed up at my cabin to ask whether I would come out of retreat the next day to arrange the tea and rice welcoming ceremony for Thrangu. They had instructions in a manual but no one on staff had actually led one, as I had. Naturally, I complied gladly, and after I returned to my cabin, I reflected that I had not felt apologetic, but actually proud of my ability to facilitate this modest protocol. I cannot claim that I have not struggled with self-denigration throughout my life, but I have had powerful lessons that counter this tendency, and they echo Jamgön Rinpoche's words to me that summer. What you have to offer is worthy. Who you are is okay.

When we got back to Brooklyn in the fall of 1985, we made plans to sell our apartment and move. It had been an unhappy place for us anyway, and we felt little attachment to it. We both began working as office temps, Mary made plans to begin graduate school, and our life resumed a semblance of normality. Apart from severe headaches, which lasted for several months, I seemed to have sustained little lasting damage from my six months of illness, a conclusion that would prove premature. I did not draw any major inference from the episode other than the obvious one that I had a genetic predisposition for this particular disorder. I have never been able to figure out definitively why I suffered such a major episode at precisely this time, although the inevitable correction in mood after the elation of encampment must have played a role. As with most subsequent episodes, there was a combination of stressors combined with a mystery factor that resists explication. I did not infer that I should change career paths and began to apply for more business manager jobs, although it was clear I was not ready to work in an independent school again. It was as if my violent divorce from the Brooklyn Quakers had left me leery of such a commitment ever again. In truth, it had broken my heart.

That winter I saw Trungpa Rinpoche again for the last time. We drove up to Karmê Chöling through a blizzard to attend a program he was leading on the unity of the buddhist and Shambhala teachings. The weather prevented many people from arriving in time for the first evening's talk, so the gathering was small. I was scheduled for kusung duty with him at the main house and helped get him settled into his sitting room before the talk. I felt very emotional to see him again, although he had changed markedly since I'd last seen him in Brooklyn. Trungpa Rinpoche's presence was always very still; now it was rock-like, unmoving. He spoke very little and his gestures were slow and deliberate. He was fully present, but also seemed detached, almost disinterested. There was much fussing with overcoats and hats, and some formal photographs were taken. Rinpoche seemed to barely register these events, as if he were observing them across a wide distance.

The talk that evening was otherworldly. The storm continued to rage and the power kept failing, plunging the room into darkness and cutting the amplification of Rinpoche's microphone. Then it would surge back on and Rinpoche would re-appear, loud and clear. He ignored these interruptions, and those of us present paid him rapt attention. He spoke of the inseparability of the buddhist and Shambhala paths, and also of the importance of establishing a capital for Shambhala society in Halifax, Nova Scotia. (He would relocate to Halifax later that year, along with his entire board of directors.) He spoke more slowly and deliberately than I had ever heard him, with long intervals of silence. And he told us that the mark of Shambhala citizens was that they were "cheerful, but strange."

By the time we got back to his residence the storm had abated, but it was bone-chillingly cold. We hurried to get Rinpoche from his car into the warm house, but to our mortification he asked for a chair to be set up outside in the fresh snow. Rinpoche, it seemed, wanted to savor winter's bite, and sat out in the freezing night in his fur hat and overcoat as various attendants took turns standing with him. A few minutes were enough for me but Rinpoche lasted half an hour or so. When he finally came into the kitchen his glasses fogged up, and he gave a big grin and finally spoke. Cool breeze of delight, he said to the gathering. It was somehow wonderful and typical—the man appreciated everything about being alive, even conditions most of us considered brutally harsh.

The next morning my shift continued and when the buzzer sounded in the kitchen it was time for me to go upstairs and help Rinpoche prepare for his day. I had not anticipated what I would say or do when I was alone in his presence but my response was instinctive— at the entrance to his bedroom I offered three half-prostrations, a formal gesture I had learned to make when entering the presence of the Kagyu princes. Although Trungpa Rinpoche never required such formality himself, my love and devotion to him were so much greater that it felt exactly the right thing to do, and he clearly understood, greeting me with a warm smile. I advanced and crouched at his bedside.

How are you? he asked kindly, looking me in the face.

My emotions were too strong and I had to look away. I'm fine, Rinpoche, I managed to say.

It was an innocuous exchange, but filled with meaning for me. I did not realize that he had already begun his slow process of disengagement from the physical world and would die in little more than a year, but I knew it was very important for me to see him again that winter. I helped him down the stairs for what would be the last time, again feeling the powerful sense of trust and confidence in me that his weight on my shoulder conveyed.

As the winter progressed, my status with the law firm where I was temping was upgraded to permanent. The business was in the process of computerizing its records, and I spent weeks adding columns of numbers to plug into the system. It was mindless, mechanical work and my imagination began to resurrect a long-dormant fantasy of writing a work of fiction. I had been reading about the history of the British secret service and started to create a story in my head about a police detective who uncovers a mole at Cambridge University, the last of the famous spies from the thirties. As the plot began to cohere in my mind, I took a yellow pad from the supply cabinet and made some notes. This would become the outline of *The Cambridge Theorem*, a novel that was eventually published in 1990.

We left the city for good in May 1986. I found a job with a testing company in Western Massachusetts, not as a business manager, but as a test writer. Truthfully we were both equivocal about the move, because we liked New York and would have preferred to stay. Also, Mary's first choice for graduate school was Columbia. Basically, the testing job was the best I could find and it was time to move on. We took rueful leave of our friends in the New York sangha, and hired Kind and Reasonable Movers, a moving company that was run by a sangha guy I knew, to bring our gear up to Northampton, Massachusetts,. I felt a combination of admiration and sympathy for him that he had chosen such a tough way to support himself, because I knew I could never do anything like that myself—more on this later.

Our stay in Northampton proved short-lived. Predictably I hated the test-writing job and Mary resolved that she would attend Columbia after all. She found an internship in New Haven, Connecticut and moved down there at the end of the summer. I stayed on in Northampton as I looked for other work and for several months we had a commuter marriage. But in contrast to my long, fruitless job search in New York, I was offered one of the first jobs I applied for—business manager at a scholarly film company at Yale University. At Thanksgiving I moved down to New Haven and into Mary's cramped apartment. And then something wondrous and unexpected happened—we got pregnant.

I knew that Mary had taken several home pregnancy tests over the years so was somewhat skeptical when she said a test had turned up positive. But there it was—a little dark ring at the bottom of a test tube on the top of our dresser, a clear positive result. We stood there speechless with happiness, holding hands and crossing our fingers that the result was not a false positive. It indeed was not, and the sentient being thus indicated, our daughter Phoebe, is now 25 years old. It meant that Mary's graduate school would have to wait, but in light of this, to us, that mattered not one whit.

One final development stands out from the end of that year. The Regent returned to Boston for a teaching visit, and I felt I ought to visit him to let him know I was okay. The encounter turned out to be what I had feared when I met him in Boston six months earlier. In a roomful of people, some of whom I knew well and some not at all, he asked me in a loud voice, So, Cape, how's the lithium?

I was on kusung duty, serving drinks to his party and managed a polite, Fine, sir.

He made a boorish remark that made everyone laugh and I withdrew quietly.

I felt no resentment or betrayal at this treatment. When I am well, I can give and take mockery with enthusiasm and knew his scorn served as both a crude gesture of affection and also an admonishment for the distress I had caused him and others, both of which were fine with me at the time. I say "at the time" because in 1985 I still acquiesced with the implication that I was to blame for my illness, that I ought to be ashamed of myself. I no longer endorse this view.

sixteen

It took me several more years before I was able to fully come out of the closet as someone who suffers from clinical depression. The most painful stigma associated with the illness is the widespread belief—typically shared by the sufferers themselves—that it represents a character flaw, rather than a metabolic disorder like diabetes or hypothyroidism. For many buddhists, there is particular difficulty in accepting the need for medication both remedially and for prevention, as if meditation practice alone ought to be enough to protect the psyche from relapse. The frequent recurrences I have suffered have dissuaded me from this view, but for years I would take phone calls from other sangha members who were tormented by the prospect of taking antidepressant medication for this very reason. I always tried to persuade them otherwise. Mercifully most depressive episodes are finite and people will eventually recover, even if they do nothing. Meditation may indeed help in this recovery process. But if you are responsive to medication (again, thankfully, most sufferers are), your recovery period will be quicker and your meditation much more effective if you take a prescribed medicine. My coming-out process was significantly facilitated by my sangha brother Roger Tucker, who started an online user group for the Shambhala community in the '90s specifically for those of us laboring under the stigma of mental illness. Tucker, a life-long survivor of bipolar disorder, is a lovable rogue who deserves much credit for establishing this cleansing space for many dozens of us.

In September 1986, after Rinpoche had relocated permanently to Halifax, he suffered both respiratory failure and cardiac arrest and essentially expired in his bedroom. As the circumstances were described to me at the time, on this particular evening Rinpoche's breathing became increasingly labored and intermittent, until it simply stopped. Heroic attempts at CPR by an ambulance crew were able to restore a pulse, but Rinpoche lay in a coma in the hospital for several days. He regained consciousness, but not the ability to move or communicate cogently, and it was likely he had suffered brain damage. He lingered in his paralyzed state for almost six months, receiving round-the-clock professional care at his home in Halifax, until progressive organ failure led to his re-admission into Halifax Infirmary in March 1987. On April 4, surrounded by his wife Diana, his dharma heir Ösel Tendzin and other senior students, Trungpa Rinpoche died.

There are many anecdotes of students' cars stalling or their clocks stopping at the precise moment when Rinpoche died. In New Haven, Mary and I experienced no such portents. However, we were very aware that as our teacher passed, new life was growing in Mary's womb, and we drove out to Long Island Sound to look at the ocean and gather our thoughts. We were sad but also grateful for having known him, and our loss was offset by the anticipated birth of our first child.

In the text of my Vajrayogini sadhana, the tantric practice I've done for almost thirty years, I keep a photograph of Trungpa Rinpoche to inspire me when I recite the deity's mantra. In it, Trungpa Rinpoche sits on his teaching throne in a brocade robe in a room filled with formally dressed people. His spectacles reflect the light from the tall windows as he looks out across the offering bowls arrayed on a shrine table in front of him—except Trungpa Rinpoche is not really looking out at anyone, because he is dead. In accordance with the instructions in his will, he is seated in *samadhi,* the traditional extended interval after death during which the consciousness of a realized teacher remains in his body, even though it has died. (The samadhi concludes when the area around the heart grows cold, as it did after three days in Rinpoche's case.) It is extremely rare for a high lama to allow his samadhi to be witnessed so publicly, but Trungpa Rinpoche was an extremely rare teacher. His trust in his students, his forfeit of his privacy and his commitment to teach continued even when he was a corpse.

I was not able to make the trip to Halifax but instead drove up to Karmê Chöling after the samadhi concluded to volunteer when

Rinpoche's body arrived. We had all known he was dying, had expected it for many months, but there was still tremendous shock and disorientation in our community as we waited for the motorcade bearing his coffin to arrive from the Burlington airport. The Regent in particular seemed to be having a hard time, and no wonder. Practically every decision was now his, and whereas some official procedures had been spelled out in Rinpoche's will, many others had not. At first, the Regent favored a funeral ceremony within ten days, but luckily, in this instance and in all the confusion that followed, there was a single authority to whom we all deferred, and this was Dilgo Khyentse Rinpoche. Khyentse Rinpoche was one of the great enlightened teachers of the twentieth century, and as head of the Nyingma lineage, the oldest school of Tibetan buddhism, his spiritual authority was unimpeachable. He had been one of Trungpa Rinpoche's most important teachers in Tibet, and now lived in exile in Nepal and Bhutan. He had visited our community several times, and we all revered him. The young, westernized lamas who frequently traveled with him had nicknamed him "Mr. Universe."

Not only did Khyentse Rinpoche scotch the idea of a swift funeral, he established the precise date for the ceremony seven weeks hence on May 26, 1987. Shamar Rinpoche also helped identify a lama in California who was familiar with the traditional procedures for preserving a teacher's body for such a length of time. Lama Ganga flew in the next day and oversaw the construction of a *dungdrom*, a special box-shaped coffin in which Rinpoche's body would be seated, packed in salt, for the next seven weeks. Every few days, the salt was replaced; in this way, Rinpoche's remains were preserved and slowly desiccated. The task of replacing the salt was an extremely sensitive one, conducted in privacy by a group of Rinpoche's closest students. It had, in fact, felt wrong to see professional funeral directors carry Rinpoche's coffin into our shrine room, and once the shrine for Rinpoche's *kudung* (body relic) was built things felt like they were properly in place. The new shrine was a splendid affair in the center of the main shrine room, surrounded in the four directions by offerings and many of Rinpoche's personal effects. Students, dignitaries and other lamas began visiting to pay their respects, and Karmê Chöling began to gear up for the biggest event in its history.

The scale of our preparations was daunting. A special cremation reliquary, known as a *purkhang*, had to be constructed of firebrick and cement on a site that could accommodate several thousand people. In addition, dozens of senior Tibetan lamas, along with their attendant monks, were expected to attend. They all had to be accommodated, fed and transported. The Karmê Chöling staff ballooned from forty to two hundred fifty, and many sangha members, including myself, moved to the area for the duration of the event. There was a run on available rental housing in the area, and the sleepy local economy suddenly surged. I quickly established that my main duties would be working in the Regent's household and helping plan the service details in what we affectionately dubbed the hotel. Providentially, Karmê Chöling had recently purchased a dilapidated apartment building in neighboring Barnet, which we now had to convert into a guesthouse for lamas and monks in record time.

The Regent's household was set up in a spacious house nearby that the owners had named "Shangri-la," which everyone thought very auspicious. Most of the members of the Regent's party were people well known to me, apart from Patrick Sweeney, an impressive young man I had not met before and who had clearly enjoyed a recent meteoric rise in the Regent's esteem. The Regent seemed especially taken with Patrick, as if he was grooming him for some special role. But it was not unusual for the Regent to be captivated by handsome and accomplished young men, and this relationship did not strike me as unusual at the time.

What did seem puzzling to me was the Regent's state of mind. By now we knew each other well and were quite candid and relaxed around each other. I had seen him melt down on a couple of occasions in Boulder, losing his temper over trifles and then expressing remorse. I had sensed the pressure of always being "on" was sometimes onerous for him, and I did not envy his life of endless exposure. But from the moment Rinpoche's body arrived at Karmê Chöling, he seemed particularly gloomy, agitated and suspicious, which I ascribed to the intensity of his grief. What I did not know then was that for more than a year the Regent had known that he was HIV positive, which in this era constituted its own sentence of death. The reminder of mortality that we all experienced at Rinpoche's passing must have been made all the more sharp for him, particularly since he had been instructed by Rinpoche not to tell anyone.

This instruction was not strictly followed and the question of precisely who knew of Ösel Tendzin's illness and when was to become a very charged one in our community. What I did notice in his household in the weeks preceding the cremation was that his mood was volatile and that he was given to angry tirades against both individuals and groups that I found shocking and upsetting. In general, the kusung is supposed to be invisible and inscrutable, although personally this had always been a distant ideal. After one particularly drunken evening, which included an extended racist rant by the Regent, I found myself too agitated to leave and ended up pacing around the empty kitchen after everyone retired. Because of the strength of my connection to him, I felt I had to respond in some way to what I'd seen and heard, although I knew such an action was also technically a breach of protocol. I sat down and wrote a poem that I left in the middle of the dining table. It contained the lines:

Civilized and decent, I find your conduct appalling.

And more pointedly, I resent the vajra bully in the lilac Cadillac.

(This was a reference to the purple rental car the Regent was using.) Eventually I went back to the main house around dawn for a few hours sleep.

The next afternoon, for reasons I no longer recall, I had to return to the Regent's house to collect something I had left behind. I was quite nervous about confronting him after the petulant note I had left the night before and thought I might be in for rough treatment. But to my surprise, the Regent seemed quite subdued, and said he had appreciated the poem. In particular, Patrick Sweeney was teasing him by calling him "VBOT," for Vajra Bully Ösel Tendzin. Clearly, there was a complex dynamic operating within the household that I did not understand. This proved to be the last kusung shift I would ever serve with him.

There were other intimations of trouble to come during these weeks preceding the cremation ceremony. A total of twenty-five thrones had to be built for the senior lamas who were expected to visit before and during the ceremony (these thrones had to be of carefully graded heights, to accommodate the Byzantine but rigid Tibetan religious hierarchies.) Shamar Rinpoche, the senior of the Kagyu princes, came and left, on the pretext that he had other engagements. (We learned later that a bitter feud had broken out between him and Situ Rinpoche over the identity of the Seventeenth Karmapa, who had been born in 1985 but not yet discovered or enthroned. The two lamas could no longer easily be in each other's presence.) The next high lamas to arrive were Gyalstap Rinpoche, whom we had not met before, and our beloved Jamgön Rinpoche, whom we were all thrilled to see again. As was often the case, the lamas gave impromptu talks to the students who gathered in the shrine room after the initial welcoming ceremony. Gyalstap Rinpoche commented that when Gampopa (the founder of the Kagyu monastic order) died, he left behind the seminal text *The Jewel Ornament of Liberation*, just as we had all of Trungpa Rinpoche's writings to inspire us. Jamgön Rinpoche, now addressing us directly in English, said he was certain Trungpa Rinpoche's reincarnation would be found soon. He also added that we had the leadership of Lady Diana, the Sawang and the Regent to support us, but this seemed like an afterthought. Tellingly, Gyalstap Rinpoche did not mention the Regent at all.

Among the Tibetans, one of the most controversial actions by Trungpa Rinpoche during his lifetime was to appoint a Westerner as his dharma heir and lineage holder. There were precedents within the Tibetan tradition for odd behavior regarding sexuality and alcohol, but a break with tradition such as this one had never happened before. Despite surface politeness, it was clear the Kagyu princes did not fully trust the Regent, and that he in turn felt threatened by them. He was older than they were and fully empowered to assume the reins of one of the largest and most influential sanghas in the West, but they were his elders in the thousand-year-old Kagyu hierarchy and enjoyed tremendous respect and authority within our community. The only non-divisive figure was the great Khyentse Rinpoche himself, to whom everyone deferred. He was expected to arrive a few days before the ceremony itself, over which he would preside.

The arrival of Khyentse Rinpoche and his accompanying lamas and monks was an extraordinary event. Khyentse himself was a mountain of a man in his late seventies, six feet seven and three hundred pounds, who wore his hair in a long, gray braid and often sported nothing other than a pair of pink cotton bloomers. Because of weakening knees, he leaned heavily on two diminutive aides who traveled with him. His accompanying lamas looked like they had parachuted in from some alternate universe. Trulshik Rinpoche had a crooked smile and no hair at all; Pawo Rinpoche, his legs buckled from years of seated meditation in a Chinese prison, wore his thick, black hair piled into a topknot; the young lamas Rabjam and Dzongsar Rinpoche seemed like MTV personalities with their sunglasses, flashing smiles and colloquial English. During the prostration practice that many of us had completed, we perform a visualization of the gurus of the Kagyu and Nyingma lineages seated on the boughs of a massive tree in front of us. After the Nyingmapas arrived to join the Kagyupas who were already in residence, you could look up from your practice and actually see the vision in the flesh— twenty of the most eminent living buddhist masters in the same place, practicing together. Such was the respect that Trungpa Rinpoche commanded in the world of Tibetan buddhism.

Although two years had elapsed since my recovery from my last depression, I was not in particularly robust psychological shape. In the run-up to the cremation many of us worked very long days and the pressure was intense. I stopped sleeping again and began to feel increasingly shaky. To my acute chagrin, I realized I needed to withdraw from my scheduled post as manager of the lama hotel and take a less active role—at least I had learned to recognize my warning signs. Thus, I spoke to my superiors and moved my gear to a nearby motel. To my eternal gratitude I was then invited to join the kasung encampment, which had been established just below the cremation site and had swollen to two hundred participants from all over North America and Europe. It felt like a homecoming for me, and I immediately felt buoyed by the sense of uplifted energy in the environment. This energy, which Rinpoche called windhorse (*lungta* in Tibetan), was palpable among the kasung, who had a sense of calm purpose leavened by humor that was largely absent amid the frenzy of the main house. The kasung were overstretched too, charged as they were with transportation, security, sanitation, crowd control and a host of other duties, but their sense of composure and confidence came as a welcome relief to me. As the day of the cremation itself approached, the sense of anticipation heightened. The day before the event, the kasung staged a formal dress rehearsal, with a young sangha member taking the place of Rinpoche's body in the palanquin carried aloft on the shoulders of the ranks of senior kasung up the steep trail to the purkhang, now gilded and decorated, at the cremation site. Someone asked Situ Rinpoche what the weather would be like the next day, and he responded matter-of-factly that it would be overcast at first, then clear and sunny, which turned out to be perfectly accurate.

That morning, the first sounds we heard were the strains of a lone bagpiper, who preceded the funeral procession through the mist. Then came the distinctive wail of Tibetan horns from the procession of monks, followed by a slow-march, honor guard of kasung and the palanquin itself, swaying beneath a silk parasol. I had not shed tears yet since Rinpoche's death but came close as the pallbearers approached and skillfully slid the tiny, silk-clad corpse into place above my head. (I was occupying a post at the base of the purkhang.) There followed a long procession as family members and senior lamas circumambulated the purkhang and threw *khatas,* or ceremonial silk scarves, into the opening in the top of the purkhang through which Rinpoche's silk-covered face could just be seen. Then the fire offering ceremonies began.

Seated in the four directions beneath canopies were the lamas from the Kagyu and Nyingma schools, Rinpoche's family members and his senior students. About two hours into the ceremony, the fire was lit by a monk from India who by tradition did not know Trungpa Rinpoche. Rinpoche's cannon boomed from the hillside and smoke, fire and ashes blazed into the sky. The time of his dissolution had truly arrived. The ceremony continued for approximately another three hours,

I truly do not remember what I did during this extended period. My shift at the base of the purkhang ended soon after the sadhanas began, and I think I may have been involved in tea service to the Tibetans. I was in such a transformed state that my memory fails me. Rinpoche describes how the experience of *adhishthana,* or the blessings of a realized teacher, can seem so tangible that they feel almost moist. After the clouds lifted and the sky turned blue and the liturgies began, I felt like I was in a sauna. My discursive mind resembled a lava lamp, my thoughts barely breaking the surface. When the miraculous phenomena began to appear (first a perfect circular rainbow around the sun, then the multi-colored clouds that drifted along the horizon in the shape of tantric symbols) I felt a smile of recognition rather than the thigh-slapping enthusiasm I'd experienced three years earlier when Rinpoche and Gerald Red Elk conjured the rainstorm and rainbow at encampment. It was a memorable experience, although I have almost no distinct memory of it.

I was snapped out of my trance-like state in late afternoon when the kusung division was rotated into service at the main house to assume responsibility for traffic flow and crowd control as the huge gathering dispersed. Within the kasung ranks there was the inevitable assumption that the kusung were a bunch of wimps in lounge suits who could handle crystal stemware but knew nothing about walkie-talkies, chains of command or heavy equipment. Well, we set out to prove our critics wrong and were soon directing ambulances, Portapotty trucks and fleets of buses through the bottleneck of the main house parking lot with aplomb. In fact, we had such a great time that we were reluctant to surrender our posts after our two-hour shift was up. I remember the senior kasung in change of logistics being visibly moved as she thanked us for our service. It was an emotional day for everyone.

I headed back up to the encampment ground as evening fell to find that my platoon had one last duty, which was to take down the flags that stood at the edge of the cremation site. This was the corny ritual that I had resisted so violently when I first went to encampment years before. The salutes and the songs finally got to me, and as the flags came down I sobbed uncontrollably because I knew I would never see Trungpa Rinpoche's face again. It was the kindest face I had ever known.

seventeen

Discrepancies surround official versions of Trungpa Rinpoche's final illness and death. Diana Mukpo relates that a combination of diabetes and high blood pressure likely led to his initial cardiac arrest, and that he eventually died from urosepsis; other sources state more baldly that Rinpoche died from cirrhosis of the liver. However, no one in our sangha likes to admit that our beloved teacher basically drank himself to death, as many alcoholics do. Because the fact is, by any clinical measure, Trungpa Rinpoche was an alcoholic. People who did not know him often demand to know why we, his students, did not individually or collectively try to curtail such a self-destructive habit. The fact is that we did, both openly and covertly. Diana Mukpo explains in her memoir that she often pleaded with Rinpoche to stop, because she feared his drinking would shorten his life. I was once in an audience with Allen Ginsberg, who tearfully begged Rinpoche not to drink himself to death as his best friend Jack Kerouac had done at the age of forty-seven. Other students would privately appeal to visiting Tibetan teachers to intercede with Rinpoche about his drinking, which tended to make the Tibetans exasperated. And we would resort to ruses, like boiling his sake to neutralize its alcohol content, which he would subvert by sneaking into the pantry to pour himself the real thing. However, such attempts at intervention were rarer than the collective compliance we all practiced, which in recovery parlance is known as enabling. But, in my opinion, such dynamics are where the similarities between Rinpoche's drinking and conventional alcoholism end.

I do not believe Trungpa Rinpoche was an ordinary man nor do I believe that his excessive drinking was alcoholism in any conventional sense. On the contrary, I believe Trungpa Rinpoche was in full control of his behavior, and that rather than produce the pathologies typical of alcoholism, his drinking actually enhanced his ability to teach and connect with others, and helped prolong his life. I also realize that these contradictory claims may seem absurd.

In part to address the criticism that greeted his drinking, Trungpa Rinpoche wrote a monograph on the topic in 1972 that he titled "Amrita as Medicine or Poison." (Amrita in Sanskrit means "nondeath" and usually refers to a complex concoction of alcohol mixed with herbs.) In the space of fifteen hundred words or so, Rinpoche first presents the range of attitudes to drinking in different cultures and eras. He then discusses the practice of what he calls "conscious drinking" in different spiritual traditions.

> Whether alcohol is to be a poison or a medicine depends on awareness during drinking…For the conscious drinker, for the yogi, the virtue of alcohol is that it brings him down to reality, so that he does not perish into nondiscriminating meditation. For him, alcohol acts as a longevity potion. Those who are overly involved with the sense that the world is a mirage, an illusion, have to be brought down out of their meditation into a state of nonmeditation to relate with men. In this state, the sights, sounds and smells of the world become overwhelmingly poignant with their humor. When the yogi drinks, it is his way of accepting the unmanifest reality of nonduality as the dualistic world of ordinary appearance. The world demands his attention, his relationship and compassion. He is glad and amused to have this invitation to communicate.

Elsewhere in the article he distinguishes alcohol from other intoxicants like marijuana, opium and LSD as the only one that enhances the sense of physicality, including the experience of hangover. This account may seem like an elaborate rationalization, but it makes lucid sense to me and succinctly describes how my teacher functioned in the world. Though Rinpoche's motor functions might have been so compromised from alcohol that he needed physical help in and out of his teaching chair, I never once had the sense during a talk that his mind or ability to communicate was impaired. He might have been unusually slow and deliberate in choosing and enunciating words, but then he was always slow and deliberate. When Rinpoche was drunk he was somehow completely himself.

There is a further clue to Rinpoche's unconventional behavior in a discussion at the end of the 1973 Seminary, when Rinpoche first introduced the tantric teachings in a careful, graded regimen to a group of senior students. Trungpa Rinpoche was a lama of the Kagyu school, whose main practice is the mahamudra tantra, which translates as great symbol. Very crudely, this tantra promotes practices that enable the adept to perceive dualistic phenomena as so vivid and luminous that they become transparent. But Rinpoche's main teacher in Tibet was Sechen Kongtrul Rinpoche, who was a lama of the Nyingma lineage, the oldest of Tibet's schools, whose ultimate practice and attainment is ati (Sanskrit) or dzokchen (Tibetan), literally "great perfection or completion." Ati masters may succeed in transcending dualistic phenomena altogether. After the final talk at the 1973 Seminary, Trungpa Rinpoche said, "Any high Maha Ati teacher…must be sybaritic. The more sybaritic they are, the more love and compassion they have for their students. That's the whole thing: they are sort of bringing themselves down instead of taking off into the whatever." This "whatever," in my view, implies disengagement from mundane reality in both figurative and literal senses. Toward the end of his life, Trungpa Rinpoche was increasingly detached from the physical realm in which we all lived. He was also prone to violent mishaps, including his car wreck and at least two serious falls, none of which I believe were accidents in any conventional sense. Rinpoche had no reason to exist apart from his commitment to teach dharma to his students, and the realm of the senses was his anchor to their world. An anecdote from my encampment experience may serve to illustrate what may seem a farfetched or contradictory notion.

A tradition had evolved from the earliest encampments of raids by "civilians" who would breach the security of the camp perimeter and steal some token item. (These raids were often encouraged and even orchestrated by Rinpoche himself.) If the culprits were caught, they were thrown into a makeshift brig fashioned from saplings and rope and made to split wood or haul water as punishment. The year I attended, a particularly flaky German guy was apprehended after a night raid and hauled before Rinpoche the next day in handcuffs. Rinpoche found these encounters hugely amusing and set about interrogating the miscreant about his motives. The German guy was quite contrite and was prepared to serve his time in the brig but pleaded with Rinpoche to remove the handcuffs, which were chafing him. Rinpoche rotated his good right hand in front of the fellow, showing him the gold Rolex watch and heavy signet rings he wore. These are my handcuffs, he said. I wear them too. This was not a frivolous remark—Rinpoche had no capacity for frivolity. He was being quite literal.

Why did Trungpa Rinpoche drink so much, even as he knew the practice was killing him? Why did he consort with so many women, even long after he lost his sexual capacity? Why did he practice such overt, controversial behaviors, knowing that many people might conclude that he was a fraud? In my view, it was for the same reason that he favored the finest of cashmere for his overcoats, the ear-splitting blast of his field cannon, the subtlest of incense for his sitting room or the most succulent meat for his plate. He was a sybarite because the realm of the senses seduced him to teach, to fulfill his karma by sticking around in our messy, neurotic world. Frequently, we were too fearful and ignorant to appreciate this, which is why visiting Tibetans would get so angry with us if we complained about Rinpoche's drinking. They understood he was sacrificing himself on our behalf, that he was a completely remarkable being of unparalleled fearlessness and compassion. They must have wondered whether we understood who he was or deserved the good fortune of having met him at all.

This explanation may be construed as further denial by an "enabler." Many people who respect Trungpa Rinpoche's teachings and even serve within his organizations prefer the formulation that his drinking and sexuality represented his "dark side," which all human beings, enlightened or not, manifest. This is a wrong view. The Trungpa Rinpoche I knew was endlessly gentle, patient and kind, but he did indeed have a dark and unpredictable side that was scary to experience. I saw him angry only once, when he (appropriately) threw the Beat poet Gregory Corso out of a talk for persistently heckling him. Corso was a fine poet but also a drunken barbarian and kept yelling things like "Smart fucker!" and "You tell 'em, Choggie." Rinpoche eventually yelled at his guards to remove him and a dark, poisonous cloud enveloped the room. During his final retreat at Mill Village in Nova Scotia, Rinpoche's behavior became increasingly erratic and tough to be around; only the closest of students were able to handle it and it was often frightening and disorienting for them. This indeed was Trungpa Rinpoche's "dark side." His drinking and sexuality were part of his playfulness, his way of communicating with the world.

After Diana Mukpo's brave memoir appeared in 2006, she was interviewed for the cover story of the *Shambhala Sun,* the national periodical on buddhism and culture that was begun by members of our community. Predictably, Diana was asked direct questions about Rinpoche's drinking and sexuality, which inevitably remain central questions about his life. Diana answered these questions candidly and persuasively, as she had already done in her book. On the subject of his alcohol use, she responded: "I think that Rinpoche probably drank because it facilitated his ability to teach in the West. I think he drank because he felt that he was able to harness more energy to teach." Of his sexuality, she said: "Rinpoche had intimate relationships in many different ways with many of his students, and the fact that he slept with different women was an expression of the intimacy that he had with people. Another thing that was important was that Rinpoche never attempted to hide anything about his behavior…I didn't really have any difficulty with it because I think that people were never exploited."

In the following issue the *Sun* published a couple of outraged letters to the editor, which I suspect were representative of a much broader response. The first writer, a woman with a PhD from Santa Barbara, California with a long and intimate knowledge of our community, made the following points: "Unfortunately, the traditions and justifications of excessive drinking kept a lot of alcoholics in the community from getting the help they desperately needed to live a sober life," and further "[Rinpoche's] sleeping with [students]…simply prolonged the adolescence of the community. I can understand how vital boundaries could have been crossed during that period, yet this old, sad story of abuse of power was exploitative and harmful to many students. Many of Rinpoche's students' marriages were torn apart in the experiment of 'openness.'" A second letter writer, comparing Rinpoche's activities to recent scandals among Christian clergy, simply called his behavior "abhorrent."

The accusations made by the first writer strike me as largely true. A significant percentage of our community has struggled with alcoholism and although a buddhist-inspired recovery group was formed in the '80s, the prevailing attitude toward drinking has typically been cavalier and permissive. And indeed, our community had a most prolonged adolescence regarding sexuality, livelihood and many other adult obligations. In this context, I think it is fair to say that the example set by Rinpoche was harmful, and I have already conceded that it is beside the point to argue that Rinpoche did not advocate that we should emulate those behaviors. But it must also be conceded that we were an immature and permissive *generation*. We were determined to break out of our parents' black-and-white movie of duty and conformity and connect with What Really Mattered and have fun while we were about it. The stability and prosperity that our parents bequeathed us, together with our sheer demographic clout, gave us our sense of entitlement. This is the culture that Trungpa Rinpoche encountered when he arrived in North America in 1970, and he responded with the courage, compassion and skill that I hope I have presented. Had he encountered a different culture, he would have reacted differently. He was always destined to be an unconventional teacher, but his particular style was determined by the historical context in which he found himself.

Different individuals who have advised me on the composition of this memoir have suggested I avoid discussion of this topic altogether, because I lack what the tantric tradition calls "the higher perceptions" and am therefore not qualified to speculate about the unfathomable behavior of an enlightened being. I cannot comply with this advice. If buddhism is to take root in Western culture, it must accommodate its norms of individual rights and personal accountability. Those of us who continue to teach within the Shambhala community are regularly confronted by sincere questions from people interested in our sangha but who are confused by Rinpoche's behavior regarding sex and alcohol. We cannot simply evade the issue. Our community has perhaps been slow to take responsibility around these topics, but it has done so. Alcoholism is recognized as an illness and recovery groups meet in most centers. And our organization recognizes that sexual relations between teacher and student are inappropriate and has banned them. All teachers at important programs in the Shambhala community are now required to read and sign a document called "Intimate Relationships with Participants" that disallows such conduct and establishes penalties for violation. These are healthy developments. Nevertheless, before our community matured to this extent, we almost perished in the early '90s over the specific issue of sexual misconduct.

In 1985, at Trungpa Rinpoche's behest, the Vajra Regent Ösel Tendzin took a blood test in which he tested positive for HIV. This development was not shared with the sangha at large. After a young man who had been one of his sexual partners got sick and also tested positive in November 1988, the Regent was obliged to admit that he was also HIV positive. The board of directors, some of whom had known since 1985 of the Regent's diagnosis and were simply crossing their fingers that he was behaving responsibly, insisted that the information be broadcast so that others among his sexual partners, and the partners of those partners, could get tested. The news spread through our community like wildfire and there was instant alarm and outrage. The Regent was on retreat in California at the time, but was scheduled to hold a community meeting within days at the Berkeley Shambhala Center. He made his first public remarks about this development in Berkeley on December 15, 1988.

The crisis that ensued evolved very rapidly and is difficult to reconstruct in all its complexity. However, as I review documents from the era, it is clear that the Regent never again struck the note of contrition that he sounded at the first Berkeley talk, and that the prospect for reconciliation that existed at that first meeting was quickly lost. The repercussions of the split that followed reverberate to this day, and the sense of loss and betrayal are still with us. Again, I have been advised by some not to discuss these events, but I feel a sense of responsibility to the history of our community and the broader history of buddhism in the United States to recount as accurately as possible what happened. My own immediate response was an urgent need to know exactly what the Regent said to the gathering in Berkeley that day, and I was fortunate to have a close friend who had attended and who was able to supply a firsthand account. I remember feeling optimistic that if the Regent accepted responsibility for what had happened and would so publicly acknowledge it, we might survive the upheaval that was bound to follow.

Among other remarks at Berkeley, the Regent said, "[T]he transgressions that have occurred in my mind and the going against the basic dharma that has occurred in my mind are completely my doing and …I take that karma on myself." He went on to say he welcomed the opportunity "to see all of you and to be able to say these things…to begin to purify whatever evil deeds or obscurations have accumulated through my own ignorance." He then discussed the transgression of vows in hinayana, mahayana and tantric buddhism and said "All of those we are involved in here." Then, in answer to a direct question about what he and Trungpa Rinpoche discussed when his illness first became known, the Regent said the following: "I do not want to use in any way the kind of exchange that happened between he and I as a way of manipulating anybody's consciousness or trying to get out of any particular wrongdoing, okay? At that time, we talked about the illness and at that time he said to me, 'It's possible for you to change the karma.' Because I was lazy and stupid at the time, I did not understand the implication of that. And thinking that I had some extraordinary means of protection, I went ahead with my business as if something else would take care of it for me. However, what he was actually talking about was more manual labor, that I should reverse the karmic propensities and reverse the karmic accumulation altogether. So that is what happened."

There were doubtless issues of personal and institutional liability that prevented the Regent from saying directly, "I continued to have unprotected sex despite the fact I was HIV positive and may have infected others, which was a big mistake" but this admission is clearly implied by his remarks. He also accepted full responsibility for his actions and says he misunderstood his teacher's advice about changing his karma. The Regent ended his talk by saying he was planning to visit Los Angeles the next day to see Kalu Rinpoche, one of the most venerable and respected Kagyu lamas in the West. He would then visit Boston to speak to a sangha gathering there.

The facilitator of the gathering with Kalu Rinpoche was the controversial figure of Karl Springer, the longtime director of external affairs for Rinpoche and a deft politician. He also happened to be the only open homosexual member of the board of directors, and the only one who remained loyal to the Regent throughout the duration of the ensuing crisis. Springer introduced Kalu Rinpoche to the audience in Los Angeles, and his remarks were basically an extended statement of support for the Regent. Although Kalu conceded that people were afraid that he might have passed his illness on to "many, many people," he expressed his belief that "there's nothing to this particular worry." By the time the Regent arrived in Boston in mid-January, however, the sense of confrontation had escalated. At a meeting held in Boston before the Regent's arrival, the eleven members of the Vajradhatu board (excluding Karl Springer) condemned the Regent's behavior in the following language: "You have used your position as Vajra Regent in order to induce others to fulfill your sexual desires," and asked him to step down because his actions had "become a source of great pain and confusion." The Regent had declined to do so. It was against this backdrop that he addressed a gathering of several hundred sangha members from all over the eastern United States and Canada at Boston Shambhala Center. I was present at this talk, in the same room where I had sought his help, bewildered and lost, four years earlier.

The Regent looked pale and had lost weight, but he spoke with clarity and vigor. He was clearly saddened by what had transpired, but he also projected a sense of both betrayal and defiance. He could not step down, he explained, because that would violate the vows he had taken with Rinpoche and also, as he later wrote "[his] heart." His account of what transpired in the fateful interview with Rinpoche had also expanded from what he had said in Berkeley. Before volunteering his updated version, the Regent cautioned us that his remarks "[were] not for the papers, okay?" (Several press reports had already appeared, and a major story would run in *The New York Times* on February 21 under the headline "Buddhists in U.S. Agonize on AIDS Issue.") The Regent said that Rinpoche told him he could change his karma and turn his illness around "on a molecular level." When the Regent asked him, "What if people want to sleep with me?" Rinpoche replied that he would not pass the illness along. He also told him not to tell anyone of his infection.

Personally, this was the turning point in my wavering support for his position. He seemed willing to transfer responsibility for his behavior to Trungpa Rinpoche, and to imply that he was merely following his teacher's instructions. The formulation "What if people want to sleep with me?" struck me as particularly disingenuous. His earlier admission in Berkeley that he had misunderstood Rinpoche's "change the karma" instruction, and the notion that rather than change his "propensities" he mistakenly assumed he had "extraordinary means of protection," had been jettisoned. Now Trungpa Rinpoche seemed to have revoked the laws of epidemiology on his behalf, which he had loyally trusted.

No one else was present during this interview, thus their precise exchange can never be known. But the evolution of a much more exculpatory version between Berkeley and Boston struck a false note. And even if the later version were true, the notion that Trungpa Rinpoche was infallible was flat wrong. Rinpoche could and did make mistakes, and admit to them. To fail to notify his sexual partners that he was HIV positive was a transgression on the Regent's part, and in Boston he sought to evade that admission. On some level, I didn't blame him. The crisis had excavated much buried resentment toward him, and some saw the opportunity to overthrow him. To most of us outside the immediate power struggle, however, the response was simple heartbreak and anguish. Very quickly, it became difficult to remain neutral—you were either with him or against him.

After the talk my instinct was to speak with him directly. Out in the lobby, he was besieged by petitioners. I approached him. His hair was very short and his skin looked translucent.

Can I talk to you? I asked.

Sure, he said. Come over to the house. (At that time, Shambhala Center owned the house next door.)

I considered saying something more, but was shoved aside by a friend from Karmê Chöling whose face was filled with fury.

How could you? he demanded, and I realized he must have been one of the Regent's uninformed partners.

Come over to the house, he said to my friend. In the end, I realized it would likely be a zoo over there, so I didn't go. I never spoke to him again.

eighteen

After the gathering at Boston Shambhala Center, I wrote a letter to the Regent saying I could no longer support him in his standoff with the board. I felt that the disclosure of his conversation with Rinpoche constituted his playing a card from his sleeve to try and trump the deserved indignation about his behavior. The letter was hard to write in light of my huge personal obligation to him, and the genuine love I felt for him. But I knew my own difficulty was a mere sliver of the tremendous pain throughout our whole community as individuals agonized over how to respond to the crisis. I sent the letter to him in Ojai, California, to where he had traveled after his Boston talk, and where he spent most of the remainder of his life.

Throughout the spring and summer of 1989, the lobbying intensified over competing narratives of blame and responsibility. The opposed power centers of Halifax and Ojai vied for control of finances and other levers of power. The sangha was split into two, and although no official poll was taken, the prevailing view among my sangha friends was that the Regent had essentially forfeited the trust necessary for continued leadership by his behavior both before and during the crisis. Hearsay and innuendo flew around the country. Competing anecdotal and documental evidence was also cited. On the one hand, Rinpoche was said to have expressed grave doubts about the Regent's status toward the end of his life, and a clause in his will counseled us "to remind him of his sanity and good behavior." On the other hand, there were many instances of Rinpoche's reaffirming his confidence in the Regent, which had been corroborated by many senior lamas. Rinpoche's will contained the statement: "Needless to say, the Regent is the regent, the dharma heir." Rinpoche could have changed his will at any time to revoke the

Regent's succession, and never did so. For everyone, it was a bewildering time. Some people left our community and joined other sanghas; others simply stopped practicing altogether.

Then in October 1989, Khyentse Rinpoche issued a letter that appeared to rule decisively in favor of the Regent. Among other declarations of support, the letter stated, "Trungpa Rinpoche appointed the Regent knowing his capacities and seeing completely his capabilities to continue his lineage. Those who are experiencing difficulties following the Regent should now realize that it is necessary...to follow Trungpa Rinpoche's instructions." Depending on your position, this letter was greeted with either jubilation or despair, since everyone deferred to Khyentse. However, leading opponents of the Regent were suspicious. They questioned why the Tibetan original of Khyentse's letter was not supplied, and distrusted the fact that it had been written after a visit from Karl Springer, the most prominent of Regent loyalists. In response, the board deputed its own delegation to visit Khyentse, as did an independent group of sangha members in Boulder.

Both the board delegation and the independent Boulder group left to meet with Khyentse Rinpoche in February 1990 and visited many other prominent lamas as well. There was also a delegation of Regent supporters traveling a similar itinerary at the same time, which led to antic encounters like the February 8 flight from New Delhi to Kathmandu on which parties from both camps occupied seats. Then on February 26, 1990 came a further shock. The Regent's wife Lila Rich read a prepared statement from him during our international Shambhala Day broadcast, which explained that he had received a further letter from Khyentse Rinpoche on February 15 instructing him to remain in strict retreat and not assume any teaching or administrative duties in the coming year. Accordingly, he was canceling his plans to lead our major programs in 1990. This bombshell made us wonder what had happened in the intervening four months to make Khyentse Rinpoche change his position so radically. Although the Regent's statement maintained that these instructions were merely to protect his health, the sangha-at-large saw the announcement as his de facto removal from power. When the text of Khyentse's February letter and the reports from the traveling delegations were finally released, the situation became clearer.

Khyentse's February letter begins with the statement, "I have received many letters expressing the concerns of your community. Since I could not reply to everyone individually, I would like to convey here the fruit of my reflection. I feel strongly that it is important that the Vajra Regent do a strict retreat, starting with this New Year of the Horse [February 1990– February 1991], and at least for the duration of this year." The letter advised that on the anniversary of Rinpoche's death, an intensive, one-week practice program be held followed by a conference in order to find "a constructive solution…to resolve the current conflicts." (This conference was planned but never held, because of wrangling over logistics.)

The delegation reports clarified that when Khyentse wrote his original October letter from Bhutan, he was not accompanied by his closest advisers and translator. The inference was that the volume of mail that Khyentse received and further communication with others more knowledgeable about the situation in North America had changed his mind.

Ironically, while all this turmoil unfolded, my own family experienced a dramatic upswing in its fortunes. The novel that I had completed in 1988 was sold to publishers in the United States and Britain for what seemed at the time outlandish sums. We were able to buy a large, comfortable house in New Haven and hire a nanny to allow Mary to resume graduate school. Almost immediately and delightfully, Mary became pregnant again and our second child, a son Jack, was born in March 1990. The pain and drama unfolding in our spiritual community was largely eclipsed by the joy and drama unfolding for our family. I was aware of the seesaw developments within our sangha stretching from southern California to Nova Scotia to India, Nepal and Bhutan, but I was largely a detached observer. We did manage one trip to the Kagyu monastery in Woodstock, New York to visit our beloved Jamgön Rinpoche. He gave our infant daughter Phoebe her buddhist name, Dawa Sangmo, or "Moon of Goodness."

The proposed reconciliation conference that spring never materialized. After some hesitation among the board, a Seminary was held at RMDC led by senior students, not Ösel Tendzin. In the meantime, a separate community developed around the Regent at Ojai, where a wealthy patron helped secure property for a dharma center. Many of those who felt most closely connected to him moved to Ojai and effectively broke with the organization administered from Halifax. Friends of mine visited Ojai during this period and returned with accounts of the Regent's remarkable spiritual development during the last summer of his life. I fully accept this, and have always believed that Ösel Tendzin was a person of remarkable attainment, and the only member of our community with the courage, devotion and depth of understanding to undertake the impossible role of Trungpa Rinpoche's successor. Around this time we also learned that he had appointed Patrick Sweeney as his dharma heir, a development that was widely anticipated.

On August 26, 1990 we visited Karmê Chöling because Jamgön Rinpoche, who had just performed the Vajrayogini abhisheka for our community, was scheduled to give a public blessing. It proved to be a momentous day, because the news arrived that the Regent had passed away the previous evening in a San Francisco hospital. Jamgön Rinpoche spoke, expressing great sadness, but also explaining that during a recent visit to him the Regent had agreed that upon his death, leadership of our community should pass to Rinpoche's eldest son, Sawang Ösel Mukpo, who at that time was twenty-seven years old and was studying in India. Jamgön Rinpoche also said the Kagyu princes and Khentse Rinpoche all endorsed the appointment of the Sawang as head of his father's organization. There was much grief in the big shrine tent but also a feeling of relief that consensus had been reached over succession. In our community, the Sawang was universally admired for his gentleness, intelligence, discipline and sense of humor. Rome also spoke to the gathering, paying tribute to the Regent, "someone I knew quite well," for his "devotion and tremendous heart." Then we all filed past Jamgön Rinpoche for his blessing. I sensed he was particularly impressed that Mary and I now had two children to hold up for his gentle touch.

The samadhi of Ösel Tendzin was witnessed at the San Francisco Shambhala Center, and according to those who were there, its outward signs were very similar to those of his great teacher. He was seated on a throne in meditation posture; his heart center remained warm for three days, and there was a strong sense of meditative presence in the room.

The Tibetan representative of Kalu Rinpoche in San Francisco, Lama Lodrö, was so impressed by these outward signs of samadhi that he brought his students to practice with the Regent's body, as did the abbot of the San Francisco Zen Center. After three days, Lama Lodrö suggested to Patrick Sweeney and other students of the Regent that they supplicate for the samadhi to end, which they did. After a few hours, bodily fluid flowed from the nose and ears and the samadhi ended. The Regent was cremated one week later at RMDC before a gathering of around five hundred people. The ceremony was accompanied by dramatic weather events, including a double rainbow highlighted in purple and yellow, the colors of Ösel Tendzin's personal seal.

Toward the end of 1990, in one of his first actions as new president of Vajradhatu, the Sawang Ösel Mukpo dissolved the existing board of directors and replaced it with a membership that was both more female and more international in numbers than its predecessor had been. This dissolution was by mutual consent, and was accompanied by a valedictory article and photograph on the front page of our newspaper the *Vajradhatu Sun,* now published from Halifax. I was filled with unexpected rage when I saw the picture of the conservative ranks of the board, the dozen or so Men in Dark Suits. How could they have failed in their responsibilities so catastrophically? How could they have allowed Rinpoche's legacy to be so traduced by their neglect, since we later learned that some had known of the Regent's illness long before the rest of us and had done nothing? The answer was obviously because they were all corrupt—that our whole organization was corrupt—and I was filled with a sense of outrage. However, what I was really projecting was a sense of shame at my own complicity, of all our complicity, how at the first hurdle of our teacher's death we had stumbled and almost destroyed what he had bequeathed us. (It was recently pointed out to me that only two members of the board had known of the illness "long before" the rest of us. Some others knew "for a little time" before the sangha-at-large. As I've explained, the issue of who knew what and when remains a highly sensitive one.)

I had had my own grave misgivings about the Regent's conduct during the preparations for the cremation. What had I done? I had written him a petulant note and gone back the next day to apologize. I had not resigned from his service, nor complained to someone like Rome, whom I trusted. My attachment to my continued status was too strong, and the implications of taking a stand too scary. And my sense of loyalty granted the Regent a wide margin for error. He had helped me profoundly at a time when my life was at a very low ebb. And Trungpa Rinpoche had appointed the guy, after all. Who was I to question his behavior? I am confident that such narratives of self-justification were common within our community around this time.

There was grandeur in Trungpa Rinpoche's vision of the human spirit, in which everyone was a potential and future buddha. But grandeur appropriated by ego easily becomes grandiosity, and I believe this was the Regent's and our collective downfall. This danger was at the very heart of our response to Rinpoche and his teachings, because of our sense of his preciousness and of our own specialness, the conviction, as his editor Carolyn Gimian wrote in the anthology *Recalling Chögyam Trungpa* (2005), "that we were the very best of the best of the new American breed of buddhists." Although Rinpoche continually undercut this arrogance, his style also directly fostered our sense that we were different, that we were special. Rinpoche saw us as subjects within an enlightened society, and himself as our monarch. Senior students were given titles as ambassadors, lords, ladies and dukes in the kingdom of Shambhala. As Rome put it cryptically in a press statement at the time of his death, Trungpa Rinpoche was "ambitious in a nonaggressive way." The way we collectively responded to that ambition led to the calamity after his death. Rinpoche placed enormous trust and faith in us and in the developments surrounding the Regent's illness and death, we saw just how far short of that trust we had fallen. We weren't "the best of the best" of anything. We were a complete mess.

There were other losses in the early '90s that added to our difficulties. In September 1991, Khyentse Rinpoche passed into samadhi in Bhutan; he had been in steadily failing health for many months. Much more shocking was the sudden death of Jamgön Kongtrul Rinpoche in April 1992 at the age of 38. Rinpoche had been traveling in a car in Sikkim in the early morning. His driver swerved to avoid a flock of birds on the wet road and the car hit a tree, killing three of the four occupants, including Jamgön Rinpoche. He was the closest to Trungpa

Rinpoche's sangha. He was attempting to mediate the increasingly bitter dispute between Situ and Shamar Rinpoches over the identity of the Seventeenth Karmapa, and was on his way to visit the leading candidate in Tibet when the accident happened. It was a particularly bitter blow for us—a further reminder, if we needed it, of impermanence—that death comes without warning.

Fortunately, in the two decades since these events, our sangha organization has stabilized and flourished. Credit is due in huge measure to the leadership of Ösel Mukpo, who since his recognition and enthronement in 1995 has been known by his formal title Sakyong Mipham Rinpoche. The Sakyong has now led the sangha for longer than its existence under his father, and under his increasingly bold leadership its membership has expanded into Latin America, Eastern Europe and Australasia. The Sakyong turned out to be exactly the kind of patient and wise leader our community needed; he spent the early '90s studying in Asia and traveling throughout North America and Europe, simply listening to what the sangha had to say. Many of us were disillusioned and stuck; the wounds from the Regent battles were still fresh. Then beginning in 1995 the Sakyong took a series of bold initiatives that decisively changed the character of our community.

In keeping with his designation by his father as Shambhala heir (the Regent was, of course, the dharma heir), the Sakyong dissolved the old Vajradhatu and created a new organization he called Shambhala International. He also declared (as his father had stressed toward the end of his life) that the buddhist and Shambhala teachings were inseparable, and whether we liked it or not, members of the former Vajradhatu community were now all "Shambhala buddhists." This change has been accompanied by a steady replacement of buddhist forms with Shambhala forms throughout our organization, changes that have been difficult for many older students to accommodate. Thus there exists a significant contingent of disgruntled older students who feel they don't have a place in the new order. Some have left to study with other teachers; others remain within the organization and complain. My own response is perhaps typical of the centrist position—I remain a loyal member of Shambhala and am active within the organization. At home my personal shrine keeps the buddhist and Shambhala components distinct, at they have always been for me, and I continue to observe those buddhist forms that Trungpa Rinpoche taught me and that remain precious to me.

Sakyong Mipham Rinpoche's teaching activity is still expanding, and it will fall to future biographers to chart his own remarkable story. Among his many accomplishments, I have been most struck by his seemingly endless patience with the accusation, which surfaces in many guises, that he is not his father and is somehow diluting or distorting his legacy. On this topic, he recently said: "You know, I am not Chögyam Trungpa Rinpoche…He was that pioneer who needed to be daring and outrageous…But because I'm a different person, and also because of what is needed right now, I feel like my role is very different. There's a quality of stabilizing and expanding. All the same, as time goes on, I think people will see more of the similarities than the differences." For my own part, I credit the Sakyong's first book *Turning the Mind into an Ally* with sharpening my basic meditation practice, which had become fuzzy and loose. I also am deeply grateful to him for allaying my fear that Trungpa Rinpoche's organization might not survive the calamities that followed his death.

A good storyteller tries not to leave loose ends, and it's appropriate that I update my account to acknowledge the status of some of its central characters. My former girlfriend Tessa, on whose account I first traveled to the U.S., remains a senior member of the New Kadampa Tradition buddhist community in England and for five years was its representative in San Francisco. Wendy Layton, whose friendship and support were crucial to my early involvement in the sangha, was for many years "communications liaison" (i.e., intelligence chief) to the president of Shambhala, Richard Reoch, in Halifax. She no longer works for Shambhala International but continues to live in Nova Scotia and is now a student of Dzongsar Khyentse Rinpoche. After Trungpa Rinpoche's death, John Perks enjoyed an unlikely second career as butler to the comedian Bill Cosby. More recently he has resurfaced as a teacher of something he calls "Celtic Buddhism," and is self-designated "seonaidh" or leader of such a community in New England.

Patrick Sweeney, the Regent's dharma heir, remains the leader of a small dharma community based in Morro Bay, California, north of Los

Angeles. In 2005 there almost arose reconciliation between the two sanghas brokered by President Reoch, a deft diplomat. This would have permitted Patrick to assume a teaching role in our community with the status of "lineage holder" similar to that of the Sakyong himself. This outcome was effectively vetoed by Diana Mukpo, Trungpa Rinpoche's widow, who wrote a strongly worded dissent to the agreement shortly after it was proposed. Thereafter, correspondence surfaced between Karl Springer and Dilgo Khyentse Rinpoche just weeks before Khyentse's death in 1991 that put the issue beyond doubt. In Khyentse's view, "neither purpose nor benefit in newly appointing a regent of the Regent or instituting a holder of the lineage of his tradition [would be served]" and it was therefore important that "any and all allegations concerning this be set aside completely." Khyentse Rinpoche also sent virtually the same letter to Patrick Sweeney and the Regent's widow Lila Rich. Some members of the Regent's sangha in California have rejoined Shambhala; it is clear there will be no official reconciliation between the two organizations.

epilogue

Five years elapsed from my first completion of this manuscript until I was able to successfully revise it into this book. During this interval, I was effectively impeded by the longest episode of clinical depression I have yet suffered and some other unsettling developments. Two of the more important assumptions upon which I based my personal evaluation of Rinpoche's legacy—that I enjoyed an enduring marriage and that I had an unconflicted relationship with alcohol—proved false. Thus during this long difficult time, I questioned my legitimacy to write any such account of my experience as Trungpa Rinpoche's student, because it seemed I had learned and understood very little. I was also unable to engage with buddhist practice in any meaningful way. Eventually, with the encouragement of sangha friends, I reconnected with dharma and recovered my sense of well-being.

After I began writing fiction in the '90s, I progressed from my desk job at Yale to teaching creative writing and composition in the English department. This was a happy development, although it came to an end when I relinquished the position to pursue lucrative textbook work. When this expired, I found myself high and dry, and took the improbable job of running a moving company in my new home of Amherst, Massachusetts. Called Four Guys and a Big Truck, the company had been started by a colleague of Mary's to give supervised work to guys in the psychiatric therapeutic community for which they both worked. I took the business over and ran it for the next ten years, eventually progressing from a workforce of psychiatric patients to guys from the recovery community and eventually to a proud group of lesbian and transgender folks. This was a colorful period that may merit its own separate account someday. Thus I transitioned from Ivy-League instructor to truck driver, furniture mover and small businessman while my children grew up in the agreeable Pioneer Valley of Western Massachusetts and attended the local Waldorf school.

As I've made clear, my commitment to meditation and the study of dharma has never protected me from recurrent episodes of depression. During these fifteen years I suffered many relapses, the most severe of which came while I was still teaching at Yale and which necessitated such heavy medication that for several weeks I could not reliably find my classroom.

Fortunately in this era I was treated by a most humble and compassionate psychiatrist who would take my panicked calls before class and pep-talk me into believing I could find the room and fake the lesson, which I managed consistently to do. This episode lasted about six months, and ended in an unusually abrupt and decisive fashion. I had recently begun my third or fourth medication switch, and was browsing a blurred magazine article as my children waited for haircuts. Suddenly, as I struggled to read, the type came into sharp and accessible focus and I lifted my head, newly aware that I was craving Coca-Cola. (For months I had to require myself to eat, because everything tasted of cotton.) I was no longer depressed, and remained symptom-free for a long time.

During the go-go years of the housing boom in the middle-aughts, my moving company thrived and expanded to four trucks and twenty summer staff. When the market went soft in late 2006 our continued survival began to look iffy. In addition, Mary and I had begun to experience more conflict than we had ever had. Compassion fatigue of living with such an unreliable partner played a role; other long-suppressed factors also arose. We entered counseling, which helped us clarify the issues if not resolve them. In 2007 I took the traumatic step of leaving my 26-year marriage for a new relationship, which then quickly ended. Shortly afterwards I consulted my accountant and agreed that the moving company had to declare bankruptcy. Because I had guaranteed all its loans personally, I had no choice but to declare individual bankruptcy also.

This cascade of loss was acutely painful, and I experienced an extended period of bereavement. I had switched careers and had begun teaching in the high school of the Waldorf school that my children had attended as elementary students. I was now living alone and subsisting on a salary so small I had to make monthly decisions between food and medication. And my mood grew worse and worse. Many people helped me survive this dark time. Colleagues at school were flexible when I needed to adjust my schedule. Sangha friends fed me and kept me company. Wendy and her husband had moved from Halifax back to New York, and I was able to spend time with her. My ex-wife was sympathetic to my plight despite her own sense of injury. And I switched psychiatrists, visited other practitioners and tried alternative therapies. Nothing helped. My insomnia had returned with a new ferocity, and I became dependent on an anxiolytic for sleep. I was also drinking a lot. After a year of living alone, I met Karen, who would become my second wife. She quickly pointed out to me what I knew but dared not admit— that I had a serious drinking problem. (In fairness to my first wife, Mary, Karen was not the first person to bring this to my attention.) So I stopped. When I stopped drinking, my depression intensified.

The next year was the most difficult of my life. I could not practice meditation effectively in this state, but I used to attend classes and talks because I knew the importance of getting out of my small apartment. It seemed like a joke that I pretended any connection to these profound truths. It was clear that I was a failure as a buddhist, a husband and father, and as a person. Suicide was not an option for me, but I wondered how I could contrive a homicide, because to die seemed like the best bet. I was such damaged goods that I could not make any commitment to Karen. When my cell phone plan expired, I could not even accept her offer to join her account.

Then a sangha friend suggested I attend a ten-day retreat at Karmê Chöling to complete my Vajrayogini practice—an outlandish notion really, because I had always found the practice difficult, even when I was well. But she persisted, arranged accommodations, and finagled me a discount, so I went. And then I recovered.

I have now been well for more than three years, my longest interval without symptoms since my twenties. I can even permit myself the heretical notion that I may be done with this demon—other depressives in later life have reported the same sense of deliverance. But I also know in my heart this is unlikely. Whatever the future holds, I have been granted a reprieve, a belated extra chance, which I continue to savor with a survivor's sense of gratitude and privilege. And determined not to squander it, I offer this memoir in tribute to my extraordinary teacher and in solidarity with all those who have been touched by the same ghastly affliction as I.

Trungpa Rinpoche was a trailblazer. In the history of buddhism, there have been a handful of such teachers who combine extraordinary attainment with the courage needed to pioneer the expansion of the dharma from one culture to the next—the Indian teachers Padmasambhava and Bodhidharma, who brought buddhism to Tibet and China respectively, are examples. Trungpa Rinpoche was another such individual. Raised in medieval isolation (when he first saw a Chinese armored car at night, he thought it was a dragon), he walked across the Himalayas to India, then traveled to England and eventually to the United States, where he taught for seventeen years. Since his death, buddhism has continued to flourish throughout the West, not as an exotic set of rituals, but as an accessible and practical path of spiritual development that is of immeasurable benefit to the world. For this, Trungpa Rinpoche and the many great teachers who came after him are responsible.

Trungpa Rinpoche was a dharma king, and the scriptures confer different titles—dharmaraja, chakravartin, mahasiddha—that recognize this highest accomplishment. Such teachers often remain aloof from their students, high on their thrones, conferring empowerments and blessings. Trungpa Rinpoche did not do this. He took off his robe and dispensed with the privileges of his status, because he saw them as obstacles to genuine communication. For the last ten years of his life, I had the privilege of being one of those who received the benefits of his generosity. He got down off his throne and sat on the rug with me, telling dirty jokes. He held my hand and showed me how to strike the ceremonial drum and offered me hot rum from his thermos flask. For all these and countless other acts of his kindness, I feel very grateful.

acknowledgements

Many individuals helped with advice and encouragement during the process of writing this book. I'd particularly like to thank the following people: Sam Bercholz, John Baker, Jeremy Hayward, Frank Berliner, Larry Mermelstein, Lodro Dorje Holm, Walter Fordham, Peter Volz, John Sennhauser, Joe Arak, Deborah Arak, Wendy Layton, Andrew Munro, Karen Johnston, Mary Tibbetts-Cape, Grace Nolan, Rosie Pearson, Deborah Schneider, Steve Tibbetts, Andrew Seear, Steve Strimer.

TONY CAPE was born in 1951 in Swansea, Wales, grew up in West Yorkshire and attended Cambridge University. After working as a journalist in Northern Ireland and England, he moved to the United States in 1977 to join the buddhist community of Chogyam Trungpa, Rinpoche in Colorado. He has also lived in Vermont, Connecticut, New York and Massachusetts. He has taught writing at Bard College and Yale University and now teaches at Hartsbrook Waldorf School in Hadley, Massachusetts. He is the author of four works of fiction.